UNLOCKING ARTIFICIAL INTELLIGENCE FOR ENTREPRENEUR SUCCESS

Practical Playbooks to Build a Smarter Business with ChatGPT and AI!

Stirling Hale

ISBN: 978-1-964520-08-7
(Paperback Edition)

Table of Contents

Introduction

Harnessing AI to Empower Your Business Journey

Welcome to a world where Artificial Intelligence (AI) isn't just for tech giants or sci-fi novels—it's for you, the business owner, the entrepreneur, the dreamer, and the doer. Whether you're bursting with ideas or waiting for inspiration to strike, this book will show you how AI can be a powerful partner in your business journey.

Have you ever thought, *"AI sounds amazing, but how could I ever use it in my business? I'm not a techie."* You're not alone. Many people believe AI is complex, expensive, and reserved for someone else. But here's the truth: AI has never been more accessible. It's no longer a luxury for big corporations. Today, small businesses, solopreneurs, and anyone willing to learn can leverage AI to save time, grow their business, be creative, and—yes—stay sane.

A Small Business Transformation

Let me tell you about Emma, a small business owner who runs a custom jewelry shop. Emma's days were consumed by managing customer inquiries, keeping track of orders, and juggling social media marketing. She'd heard of AI but assumed it was way too complicated for her.

One day, Emma decided to take a leap and try ChatGPT. She started small—writing a simple prompt like:

> *Write a friendly email response for a customer asking about the materials used in our handmade necklaces.*

Within seconds, ChatGPT generated a polished, professional email that Emma could use immediately. It saved her time and made her customer communication shine.

Over time, Emma began experimenting with AI for other tasks—automating her social media posts, managing inventory, and even creating personalized marketing campaigns. The transformation wasn't just in her business—it was in her confidence. Emma discovered that AI wasn't a replacement for her creativity or hard work—it was the partner she didn't know she needed, amplifying her efforts and unlocking her full potential.

Why This Book Is Different

This book isn't just about concepts—it's about action. You don't need to be a tech wizard or have a huge budget to benefit. Most of the tools we'll explore are free or very affordable. Whether you're:

- A small business owner juggling multiple responsibilities,
- A solopreneur wearing all the hats,
- A team leader looking to boost productivity, or
- Someone simply curious about AI,

This book is your toolkit for success, packed with practical strategies you can implement immediately. By the time you finish, you'll not only understand how to use AI effectively—you'll feel confident leveraging it to grow your business, spark creativity, and even reclaim some sanity along the way.

What Is a Prompt?

Prompts are the secret handshake between you and AI—simple instructions that unlock its power to generate ideas, solve problems, and save you time. Think of them as your direct line to innovation, enabling you to get exactly what you need from tools like ChatGPT.

> *Write an engaging Instagram caption for a small yoga studio promoting a new beginner-friendly yoga class, emphasizing relaxation and stress relief.*

In this book, you'll learn how to craft prompts that not only get the job done but are tailored to your business's unique needs. The possibilities are endless—and as you'll discover, they hold the power to transform how you work.

Playbooks and Exercises: Your Tools for Success

In this book, you'll find two key tools to guide your journey with AI: **playbooks** and **exercises**. Together, they create a powerful framework to help you implement AI effectively in your business. Let's break down what each one does and how they work together.

What Are Playbooks?

Think of **playbooks** as your strategic blueprint. They provide step-by-step instructions for tackling specific business challenges using AI, making them ideal for implementing big-picture solutions. Whether you're looking to streamline customer service, optimize workflows, or create a personalized marketing campaign, playbooks give you the full game plan to succeed.

Playbooks are practical, detailed, and reusable. Each one is designed to:

- Address real-world challenges.
- Offer clear, actionable steps.
- Be adapted to your unique business needs.

Here is an example of a Playbook:

Streamlining Customer Responses

Objective: *Streamline customer communication by creating automated responses for frequently asked questions. This ensures fast, polished replies that improve customer satisfaction while saving time for your team.*

Steps:

1. *Identify the five most frequent questions from your customers.*
2. *Write draft prompts to ask ChatGPT for polished responses.*
3. *Test these responses with your team for clarity and tone.*
4. *Save finalized answers in a shared document or integrate them with AI tools like ChatGPT plugins.*

Throughout the book, you'll see playbooks highlighted with a consistent format and icon, making them easy to spot and apply.

What Are Exercises?

While playbooks offer the strategy, **exercises** focus on practice. Exercises are shorter, hands-on activities designed to build confidence and help you experiment with AI tools in a focused way. They guide you through specific skills, such as crafting effective prompts or testing an AI feature.

Think of exercises as your personal AI lab, where you can:

- Experiment with small-scale tasks.
- Develop a deeper understanding of how AI works.
- Gain quick, actionable wins.

This is an example of an Exercise:

Practice Crafting Prompts

Objective: *Now, imagine you want to learn how to write better prompts. An exercise might guide you to take a vague request, such as "Help me improve my marketing," and refine it into a clear, targeted prompt, such as "Suggest three social media strategies for a bakery targeting health-conscious customers."*

Steps:

1. ***Start with a vague prompt like***: *"How do I grow my business?"*
2. ***Refine it into a specific prompt***: *"What are three marketing strategies for a bakery targeting health-conscious customers?"*
3. ***Compare*** *the AI responses and reflect on the differences.*

Exercises are bite-sized, approachable, and perfect for testing ideas or building foundational skills.

How Playbooks and Exercises Work Together

The key difference between playbooks and exercises is their scope and purpose:

- **Playbooks** = Strategy: Comprehensive, multi-step frameworks to solve problems or implement AI-powered solutions.
- **Exercises** = Practice: Focused activities to reinforce skills or explore concepts in a hands-on way.

By combining playbooks and exercises, you'll learn through action—whether tackling a big business challenge or sharpening individual skills. Together, they empower you to integrate AI into your workflow, step by step.

Keep an Eye Out for Nerd Nuggets

Sprinkled throughout this book, you'll discover **Nerd Nuggets**—quick, bite-sized pieces of wisdom designed to enhance your understanding of AI and help you crush it in the real world. Whether it's a practical tip, an insightful fact, or a quirky reminder, these nuggets are here to make your AI journey smoother and more enjoyable.

Think of them as the trail mix of this book: packed with energy, easy to digest, and maybe even a little nutty. Each Nerd Nugget is crafted to:

- Offer a fresh perspective on AI concepts.
- Highlight real-world applications you might not have considered.
- Deliver actionable insights to boost your success.

Automating Tasks with AI

Did you know that automating repetitive tasks with AI can save you up to 20% of your workweek? That's like getting an extra day to focus on what really matters!

Keep an eye out for these gems as you read. They're your pocket-sized power-ups, ready to help you navigate the vast universe of AI with confidence—and maybe even a smile.

Hungered for Feedback

I truly value your input as a reader, and your feedback helps me improve my work for future editions. If you have any thoughts, suggestions, or even constructive criticisms, I would love to hear from you. Please feel free to reach out to me at:

feedback@wizardrypress.com

Whether it's a question, a new idea, or just a note on what worked well or didn't, your voice matters and is greatly appreciated. I'm hungry to hear it!

What's Next?

Congratulations! You've taken the first step into the world of AI for business. From understanding prompts to leveraging playbooks and exercises, you're now equipped with the foundational tools to start your journey. Think of this book as your personal AI guide—packed with practical strategies, actionable insights, and a touch of nerdy wisdom to help you succeed.

In Chapter 1, we'll break down AI into simple, relatable terms—what it is, how it works, and why it's becoming a game-changer for businesses of all sizes. By the end of the chapter, you'll have a solid understanding of AI's potential and how it can supercharge your business, setting the stage for the hands-on strategies to come.

The possibilities are endless, and the next chapter is your launchpad. Let's get started—your AI-powered future awaits!

Chapter 1: Demystifying AI

Understanding the Basics Without the Jargon

Welcome to the world of Artificial Intelligence (AI), where cutting-edge technology meets practical applications to transform how businesses operate. In this chapter, we'll break down the fundamentals of AI in a way that's approachable and relatable, leaving the jargon behind. Whether you're a tech enthusiast or completely new to AI, this chapter will equip you with a clear understanding of what AI is, how it works, and why it matters for your business.

We'll explore how AI mimics human intelligence, learns from data, and evolves over time. You'll see real-world examples of AI in action, from predicting customer preferences to streamlining day-to-day operations. Most importantly, we'll address the common myths that might be holding you back from embracing this game-changing technology. By the end of this chapter, you'll not only understand the basics of AI but also recognize its incredible potential to empower your business.

1.1 What is AI?

At its simplest, Artificial Intelligence (AI) is the ability of computers to mimic human intelligence—learning from data, making decisions, and improving over time. AI can take in vast amounts of data, learn from it, and then make predictions or take actions based on that knowledge. In short, AI is about teaching machines how to think and act on their own, without constant human guidance.

You've probably interacted with AI without even realizing it. It's in your phone's voice assistant, your email's spam filter, or even in the way Netflix suggests your next favorite show. These tools use AI to learn your preferences and make decisions based on that data, all in the background. But AI is so much more than just these conveniences—it's a powerful tool that can revolutionize your business operations.

AI isn't just about making computers "smarter"—it's about helping businesses run more efficiently. For example, imagine a bakery that uses AI to track which pastries sell best during certain times of the year. The AI doesn't know anything about pastries when it starts. But as it gathers data—like customer orders, time of year, and sales patterns—it begins to learn what works. The AI can then suggest the best times to bake specific pastries or even send out personalized offers to customers, all based on the knowledge it's gained.

This process is called machine learning. Over time, the more data the AI receives, the smarter it gets. Just like a baby learns new things as she grows, AI learns and improves the more it interacts with data. Think of AI as a growing learner with a powerful brain, constantly improving as it processes more information. Unlike a baby, though, AI doesn't need breaks or naps—it just keeps working and learning, getting better at what it does with every new piece of information.

AI doesn't just live in your phone or your favorite apps; it's everywhere. For businesses, AI can help automate tasks, streamline operations, and even predict future trends. It's a tool that can help small businesses grow without requiring a huge budget or a technical background.

1.2 How AI Can Supercharge Your Business

Imagine having a tireless assistant at your side, boosting productivity, tailoring marketing efforts, and automating routine tasks. AI can send personalized offers to customers at just the right time, help you build lasting relationships, and allow you to focus on what truly matters. AI isn't just for big corporations with hefty budgets—it's accessible and affordable for businesses of all sizes.

AI can help small businesses in many ways:

- **Automate customer support**: Chatbots powered by AI can handle routine customer inquiries, freeing up your time to focus on other tasks.

- **Personalize marketing**: AI can analyze customer data to suggest personalized offers or promotions, making marketing efforts more targeted and effective.

- **Analyze business data**: AI can process and analyze data from sales, customer behavior, and market trends, helping you make smarter, data-driven decisions.

- **Predict future trends**: By analyzing historical data, AI can predict future sales trends, helping you plan ahead for your business.

By the end of this book, you'll not only understand what AI is, but how you can apply it to drive business growth. Whether using AI for customer insights, managing your online presence, or simply automating customer responses, the tools you'll discover here will help you grow your business without requiring a technical background.

1.3 Dig Deeper into Artificial Intelligence (AI)?

At its core, **AI** is the ability of computers to mimic human intelligence—learning from data, making decisions autonomously, and improving over time. It's woven into our daily routines, often without us even noticing—from virtual assistants on our phones and search engines that know just what we're looking for, to recommendation engines suggesting our next favorite show.

In the business world, AI is a game-changer. Small businesses are using it to **automate customer service chats**, streamline inventory management, explore new products and services, personalize marketing efforts, and so much more. This technology is proving to be a powerful tool for anyone aiming to grow efficiently, whether it's a startup or an established small business.

To illustrate AI in action, meet **Bob**, a small-town florist who spent more time with petunias than pixels. One day, he received a mysterious email suggesting he should "digitize his operations." Bob thought it meant turning his flowers into pixels. Little did he know, it was the start of an adventure with AI that would transform his humble shop into a blooming online empire.

At first, Bob was skeptical—AI sounded like something out of a sci-fi movie, not something for a rose lover like him. He also assumed AI was only for big tech companies, not for small businesses like his. But once he dipped his toes into the world of AI, he found it wasn't about robots taking over his flower arrangements—it was about making his life easier and, more importantly, enhancing the experience for his customers, from personalized service to faster response times.

1.4 Understanding AI and Its Business Potential

Now, let's dive into how **AI works** and what makes it such a game-changer for businesses. AI empowers machines to mimic human intelligence, learning from each interaction to make smarter, more accurate decisions over time. Think of it as the **brainpower** behind your computer's actions—taking data, learning from it, and then applying that knowledge in real-world scenarios.

One key area within AI is **machine learning**. Picture it as giving your computer a fishing rod and teaching it to fish rather than just handing it fish daily. Machine learning allows systems to identify patterns and make decisions based on data, which can be a huge advantage for business insights. For example, machine learning turns raw data into actionable intelligence, like predicting market trends or customer preferences. This isn't just guesswork; it's like having a **crystal ball** that helps you make informed decisions to grow your business.

AI is revolutionizing industries left and right, bringing unprecedented benefits in fields like **retail**, **healthcare**, and **finance**. In retail, for instance, AI creates personalized shopping experiences, making customers feel as if they have a personal shopper. In healthcare, AI-driven predictive analytics enhance patient care by anticipating needs before they arise. In finance, AI serves as a diligent watchdog, enhancing security and identifying fraud before it happens. This technology isn't limited to just these sectors—it's reshaping business operations across the board.

The benefits of AI for business growth and efficiency are akin to finding a treasure map to success. It enhances customer engagement by offering tailored marketing strategies, streamlines operations, and provides deep insights that help you make smarter, growth-driven decisions. AI is not just a tool; it's a **powerful ally** in shaping a successful business.

AI's Crystal Ball

AI doesn't actually see the future, but its predictions can feel magical. By analyzing patterns in data, AI makes informed predictions—such as forecasting your favorite pastry before you even walk into the bakery.

1.5 Breaking Down AI Myths

Let's address a few common myths that might be holding you back from embracing AI for your business:

Myth 1: AI is Only for Big Corporations and is Too Expensive

AI has traditionally been associated with tech giants, but that's changing fast. Today, many AI solutions are specifically designed for **small businesses**. **No-code platforms** and **beginner-friendly tools** are making it possible for anyone—from solo entrepreneurs to small business teams—to harness AI without a tech team. Whether it's automating customer support, creating personalized marketing, or analyzing data, AI tools are becoming as accessible as any business software.

Consider AI-powered marketing tools like **HubSpot** or simple chatbot integrations like **ChatGPT**. These tools are already being used by small, independent businesses and can be set up without advanced technical knowledge. Small businesses across industries—like boutique shops, local services, and freelancers—are adopting AI to stay competitive and improve efficiency.

Myth 2: AI is Complex and Requires Advanced Technical Skills

The idea that AI is prohibitively expensive and complicated used to be true, but now, affordable options abound. Many AI services offer flexible pricing, allowing small businesses to start small and expand as they grow. Some tools, like **Canva's AI-powered design features**, offer free tiers, while others provide **pay-as-you-go pricing** or monthly subscriptions designed to fit within a small business budget.

Additionally, AI doesn't have to be an all-or-nothing investment. Businesses can start by automating a single function, like **customer service** or **social media scheduling**, and gradually explore other areas as they see value. For example, using AI to automate email responses or track customer feedback is a cost-effective way to start benefiting from AI without heavy upfront costs.

Myth 3: AI Replaces Human Jobs

AI is often feared as a job-stealing force, but in reality, it's a **supportive or augmenting tool** that elevates human roles rather than replaces them. The media has fueled some of these fears with headlines like "300 Million Jobs Expected to Disappear in the Next 5 Years Due to AI" or

"Software Engineers Will Become Obsolete as AI Writes Its Own Code." While these headlines grab attention, they fail to tell the full story—and they're not true.

Take the tech industry, for example. Early reports warned that AI would make computer programmers obsolete, painting a bleak future for the profession. However, the reality is quite the opposite. AI has not only transformed how developers work—streamlining debugging, automating repetitive tasks, and boosting efficiency—but also created a higher demand for programmers. Companies now actively seek professionals to build, maintain, and improve AI-driven tools and systems.

In fact, according to the **2025 Stack Overflow Developer Survey**, 64% of developers view AI as an asset, not a threat (https://survey.stackoverflow.co/2025/work#5-is-ai-a-threat-to-your-job). These tools allow professionals to shift their focus from mundane coding tasks to more creative and high-impact work. AI isn't replacing programmers; it empowers them to tackle bigger challenges and create greater value.

Think of AI as a tool that handles repetitive, time-consuming work. Just as calculators and computers didn't eliminate the need for accountants, they enhanced their ability to focus on strategic financial planning. Similarly, the invention of cars sparked fears of obliterating the horse-and-buggy industry but instead created entirely new industries—from mechanics and automotive engineers to highway construction and fuel services.

Even simpler tools like the power drill didn't replace handymen but empowered them to work faster and handle more complex projects. AI follows the same trajectory, freeing people to focus on creativity, problem-solving, and strategic thinking.

Rather than taking jobs away, AI reshapes them, enabling professionals to spend more time innovating and less time on repetition. As we've seen with past technologies, initial fears of job loss often gave way to a wave of new opportunities. Similarly, AI is paving the way for fresh roles and specialties, allowing people to "step up the ladder" into more impactful and fulfilling work while opening doors to entirely new industries.

Rather than taking jobs away, AI reshapes them, enabling professionals to spend more time on innovation and less on repetition. As we saw with past technologies, like the shift from horse-drawn carriages to automobiles, initial fears of job loss gave way to a new wave of opportunities. Similarly, AI is paving the way for new roles and specialties, helping people **"step up the ladder"** into more impactful and fulfilling work.

1.6 Embrace Change: Updating Capabilities to Stay Competitive

As AI reshapes industries, small businesses that adapt and grow with the technology position themselves to thrive in a rapidly changing marketplace. While AI takes over repetitive tasks, it demands businesses that can effectively integrate these tools into their operations. Staying competitive isn't just about keeping up; it's about innovating ahead of the curve.

History shows us that businesses that adapt to new technologies create more value and opportunities. When cars replaced horse-drawn carriages, companies that shifted to manufacturing or servicing automobiles found themselves at the forefront of a booming industry. Similarly, as AI becomes integral to business processes, organizations that build the right capabilities will gain an edge.

Here's how to get started:

- **Identify Opportunities**: Highlight specific areas where AI can streamline your operations—whether it's automating customer support, personalizing marketing, or analyzing sales trends.
- **Invest in Training**: Provide your team with accessible AI education through free or affordable platforms. Equip them with basic knowledge of how these tools can be applied to their roles.
- **Focus on Human Strengths**: Prioritize tasks that AI can't replicate—like customer relationships, strategic planning, and creative problem-solving.

By viewing AI as a partner, small businesses can turn disruption into opportunity, gaining a competitive edge while building resilience for the future.

1.7 ChatGPT Unpacked: A Tool for Every Entrepreneur

Imagine having an assistant who never sleeps, doesn't require a salary, and always has the right words at their fingertips—that's **ChatGPT**. This clever tool is like a **Swiss Army knife** for your business, capable of processing language as naturally as you would in a coffee conversation. At its heart, ChatGPT is built on **natural language processing (NLP)**, a bit of tech wizardry that allows it to understand and respond to customer needs with uncanny accuracy.

Consider this: you receive a flood of customer inquiries daily, each requiring thoughtful responses. Traditionally, you'd need a small army of customer service reps to keep up. ChatGPT can automate these interactions with rapid-fire precision, churning out consistent, on-brand replies to common questions. This frees up your human staff to handle more complex issues, adding a layer of efficiency to your team.

Ever dreamed of a **virtual assistant** to manage your scheduling woes? ChatGPT can do that too, organizing meetings and reminders without breaking a sweat. And when it comes to marketing, ChatGPT is a **creative powerhouse**. It can generate fresh content ideas, draft posts, and even capture your brand's voice in its messaging. It's like having a **marketing genius** on call 24/7, ensuring your content stays engaging and relevant.

Recent versions of ChatGPT can remember your previous sessions, recall key details you've shared, and even analyze uploaded documents or images—making it a true business assistant rather than just a chat interface. These improvements make ChatGPT even more capable in real-world business settings, which we'll explore next.

In the real world, ChatGPT is already making waves across various business contexts. From handling a barrage of emails for online retailers to managing scheduling in corporate offices and powering chatbots for common queries, ChatGPT is streamlining operations and enhancing customer experiences across industries.

1.8 Overcoming the Fear of AI Complexity

Let's face it: AI can sound as intimidating as trying to understand the inner workings of a jet engine when all you want is a smooth flight. But fear not—AI isn't as complex as it seems. Think of algorithms as recipe-followers, taking clear instructions to deliver results.

Getting started with AI doesn't require advanced technical skills or expensive software. Follow these steps to ease into AI adoption:

- **Start with a Specific Need**: Identify one area of your business that could benefit from automation or AI support, such as automating customer inquiries or streamlining inventory tracking.
- **Choose Simple Tools**: Platforms like ChatGPT, Zapier, or Canva's AI-powered design features offer beginner-friendly solutions.
- **Experiment and Learn**: Begin with small-scale projects and refine as you go. For example, use ChatGPT to draft email responses or analyze customer feedback to uncover trends.

The key is to start small and build confidence as you experience the benefits AI can bring to your business.

1.9 AI Without Coding: The No-Code Approach

The no-code movement is making AI approachable for everyone. Platforms like **Zapier**, **Bubble**, and **Airtable** offer easy-to-use, drag-and-drop features to help automate tasks or build apps without technical knowledge. These solutions make it possible to innovate quickly and cost-effectively.

Consider a startup that lacked the resources to develop a product quickly; with no-code tools, they brought their concept to market faster. Small business owners have also used no-code platforms to streamline operations, saving both money and time.

The best way to understand AI's potential is by connecting with communities that are already exploring these tools. Start small by taking the following steps:

Call-to-Action

Look up AI-related communities or forums where you can connect with like-minded people. Join one group, introduce yourself, and share your goals. This network will provide valuable support as you explore AI.

1.10 Building Confidence in AI Utilization

When adopting AI, it's normal to feel a mix of excitement and trepidation. AI tools on the market are rigorously tested, and they work reliably to support your business. Engaging in simple exercises can help you understand AI's potential.

By addressing common concerns, engaging in practical exercises, celebrating small wins, and building a network, you can approach AI confidently and make it an integral part of your business success.

Identifying AI Opportunities in Your Business

Objective: *Identify areas in your business where AI can save time, streamline workflows, and deliver quick wins to boost your confidence and efficiency.*

Not sure where to start? Begin with one area that feels most time-consuming or overwhelming in your day-to-day operations. If you're unsure, look for low-hanging fruit—simple, repetitive tasks that are easy to automate and can deliver quick wins. Starting small helps build momentum and confidence as you explore AI solutions.

Steps:

1. ***Identify Key Challenges:*** *Take a moment to think about the areas in your business that feel time-consuming, repetitive, or difficult to manage. These are often ripe for AI solutions.*
2. ***List High-Impact Tasks:*** *Identify tasks that follow predictable patterns or repetitive workflows, such as:*

    - ***Customer Service:*** *Automate responses to FAQs with tools like ChatGPT, reducing response times and freeing up your team for complex issues.*
    - ***Content Creation:*** *Generate blog posts, captions, or emails with AI tools like ChatGPT.*
    - ***Personalized Marketing:*** *Use AI analytics to segment your audience and tailor marketing messages, improving engagement and conversion rates.*

- ***Social Media Management**: Automate post scheduling and analyze engagement patterns using tools like Buffer or Hootsuite.*
- ***Sales Forecasting**: Analyze past sales data with AI tools to predict trends and plan for the future.*
- ***Data Analysis**: Uncover trends and insights with AI-powered visualization tools.*
- ***Recruitment**: Streamline hiring by using AI tools like Workable to screen resumes and shortlist candidates efficiently.*
- ***Customer Feedback Analysis**: Analyze reviews or surveys to uncover trends and areas for improvement.*

3. ***Research AI Solutions**: Explore AI tools available for each identified task. Look for beginner-friendly, affordable options that align with your needs.*
4. ***Choose One Task to Automate**: Select a single task to focus on as a pilot project. For example, automating customer service responses with ChatGPT or streamlining social media scheduling.*

***Implement and Evaluate**: Set up the chosen AI tool and monitor its effectiveness. Gather feedback from your team or customers to refine the process.*

1.11 Summary

In this chapter, we've demystified Artificial Intelligence, showing how it mimics human intelligence, learns from data, and makes smarter decisions over time. For small businesses, AI is a game-changer—it empowers organizations to automate tasks, personalize customer experiences, and gain insights that drive growth.

We also addressed common myths, such as AI being too expensive, complex, or a threat to jobs. The reality is that AI is affordable, accessible, and an incredible partner in enhancing human capabilities. It's not about replacing people; it's about freeing them to focus on creativity, strategy, and meaningful customer engagement.

Here's what you can take away:

- AI is a powerful ally for businesses of any size.
- Starting small with specific tools or tasks can lead to big results.
- Updating your team's capabilities and focusing on human strengths will ensure your business thrives in an AI-driven world.

With these foundational concepts, you're now ready to explore specific tools and applications that can integrate AI into your business journey. Let's dive in and discover what's possible.

Chapter 2: Craft ChatGPT Prompts That Spark Your Inner Genius

Building a Strong Foundation to Transform Your Ideas into Action

Crafting effective prompts is the foundation of successful collaboration with ChatGPT. Think of prompts as the instructions you give to a highly capable assistant—clear, specific guidance ensures accurate, relevant results. In this chapter, we'll explore the building blocks of a great prompt, focusing on clarity, context, and intent. These principles will help you set the stage for productive interactions with ChatGPT, whether you're brainstorming creative ideas, gathering information, or solving complex problems.

By the end of this chapter, you'll understand how to craft prompts that are actionable and precise, allowing you to unlock the full potential of ChatGPT. These foundational skills will serve as the groundwork for the advanced techniques we'll explore in the following chapters.

2.1 ChatGPT as Your Knowledgeable Team

When working with ChatGPT, I see myself as a team lead overseeing a highly skilled and versatile team. This "team" has access to vast knowledge and can contribute meaningfully to every aspect of a project—from brainstorming ideas to providing detailed execution plans. However, like any team, its effectiveness depends on my ability to lead and guide it effectively.

As the team lead, my role is crucial. I need to define the vision, set clear goals, and provide constructive feedback to ensure we're aligned and moving in the right direction. I must also guide the team, steering it toward the goal while helping to navigate challenges and overcome obstacles that arise along the way. By setting a clear purpose and refining inputs as we progress, I can fully leverage ChatGPT's unique capabilities.

Importantly, just as I can lead my team to execute tasks, I can also turn to it for help in defining the vision, clarifying goals, or exploring other aspects of the project. By collaborating with ChatGPT, I transform it into a true partner—not just a tool for carrying out tasks but an active contributor to shaping the project's direction and strategy.

Ultimately, the success of any project depends not just on the team's skills but on how well I manage the collaboration—shaping the flow of ideas, clarifying ambiguities, and steering the effort toward the desired outcomes. ChatGPT is no different: the better I lead, the better the results I achieve.

2.2 Could You Be More Vague?

At the heart of every successful interaction with ChatGPT lies a great prompt. A great prompt is clear, specific, and purposeful. Without these elements, responses may lack focus, relevance, or actionable value. Crafting effective prompts is about guiding ChatGPT like you would a team member by providing the right level of detail, context, and direction.

Let's break down the essential qualities of a great prompt:

Clarity

A vague prompt leads to broad or generic responses. Consider if you were asked:

What's the deal with marketing?

That question could be interpreted in countless ways. For example:

- *Do you mean marketing trends, strategies, or challenges?*
- *Do you want help with your business's marketing plan or a specific tactic like social media?*
- *Are you frustrated with marketing and need to vent?*
- *Are you asking for an overview of marketing as a concept?*

ChatGPT doesn't guess your intent—it works with what you give it. So be specific. To get a focused response, aim for precision. For example:

Provide three marketing strategies for a bakery specializing in organic sourdough bread to attract health-conscious customers.

Think Like a Translator

When crafting prompts, imagine you're translating your thoughts into instructions for someone unfamiliar with your context. The clearer and more precise your "translation" is, the better the results. ChatGPT thrives on specificity, so treat it like a teammate eager to help—once they understand what you need.

Context

Have you ever felt like someone dropped you in the middle of a conversation? No context, no background, just fragments of a situation that leave you piecing it together or making assumptions. That's how ChatGPT *feels* when prompts lack context. It performs much better when given the full picture.

Without context, example:

What are some good ways to attract customers?

With context example:

I run a bakery specializing in organic sourdough bread. What are three ways to attract health-conscious customers?

Intent

Defining the purpose of your prompt helps ChatGPT determine the type of response you're looking for. Whether you want ideas, a step-by-step guide, or a creative solution, stating your intent ensures the result matches your expectations.

Unclear intent example:

Help me with social media

Clear intent example:

Suggest three Instagram post ideas to promote my bakery's fresh sourdough bread to local customers.

Even with these examples, it's worth noting that what seems "clear" at this stage might still be refined further. As we move through the chapter, we'll explore how to dig deeper into prompts, adding layers of context and precision to get even better results.

You'll create prompts that generate highly relevant and useful responses by combining clarity, context, and intent.

2.3 Building Blocks of Effective Prompts

Now that we've covered the essential qualities of a great prompt let's look at how to structure your prompts effectively to get the best results. A well-structured prompt typically includes three components:

Context

Provide relevant background information so ChatGPT understands the scope and purpose of your request. For example:

I run a bakery specializing in organic sourdough bread.

Task

Clearly state what you want ChatGPT to do. Be specific about the output you're expecting. For example:

Suggest three creative marketing ideas.

Tone/Style

Specify the desired tone or style of the response if it's important. For example:

Keep the tone friendly and casual.

When combined, these components create a prompt that is precise, actionable, and tailored to your needs:

I run a bakery specializing in organic sourdough bread. Suggest three creative marketing ideas to attract health-conscious customers, keeping the tone friendly and casual.

Crafting the Perfect Prompt

***Objective**: Create effective prompts that generate clear, relevant, and actionable responses from ChatGPT.*

***Steps**:*

1. ***Define the Task**: Start by identifying what you need help with. Is it generating ideas, gathering information, or solving a problem? Be specific*
   ***Example**: "I want ChatGPT to suggest marketing ideas for my business."*

2. ***Add Context**: Include any relevant background information to provide ChatGPT with clarity about your request.*
   ***Example** "I own a bakery specializing in organic sourdough bread."*

3. ***Specify the Output**: Clearly describe the type of response you're expecting, such as step-by-step instructions, creative ideas, or an analysis.*
   ***Example**: "Suggest three marketing ideas to attract health-conscious customers."*

4. ***Refine the Tone or Style**: If necessary, specify the tone or style you want in the response.*
   ***Example**: "Keep the tone friendly and casual."*

5. ***Combine and Review**: Put all the components together and review your prompt for clarity, context, and intent.*
   ***Final Prompt**: "I own a bakery specializing in organic sourdough bread. Suggest three marketing ideas to attract health-conscious customers, keeping the tone friendly and casual."*

2.4 Types of Prompts

Different tasks call for different types of prompts. Understanding these types can help you tailor your requests more effectively:

Informational Prompts

Use these to gather facts, insights, or explanations. For example:

What are the benefits of organic bread compared to conventional bread?

Creative Prompts

Use these to brainstorm ideas or generate unique content. For example:

Suggest five fun names for a seasonal sourdough loaf featuring cranberries and walnuts.

Instructional Prompts:

Use these to get step-by-step guidance or how-to instructions. For example:

Provide a step-by-step guide to creating an Instagram Reel to promote fresh sourdough bread.

Analytical Prompts

Use these to assess trends, evaluate data, or explore hypothetical scenarios. For example:

Analyze the pros and cons of offering a subscription box for a bakery.

Practice Crafting Prompts.

Now it's your turn! Practice crafting prompts for each of these types. Use a business or project you're working on as inspiration, or start with the examples below:

- ***Informational**: "What are the key health benefits of [product or service]?"*
- ***Creative**: "Suggest [number] unique ideas for [specific task]."*
- ***Instructional**: "Give me a step-by-step guide to [process or goal]."*
- ***Analytical**: "Evaluate the potential impact of [strategy or decision]."*

Take a moment to write your prompts and review how well they align with clarity, context, and intent.

2.5 Summary

Congratulations! You've now mastered the essentials of crafting effective prompts, including the importance of clarity, context, and intent. With these tools, you can confidently guide ChatGPT to deliver meaningful and relevant responses. Remember, a well-crafted prompt is just the beginning—it sets the stage for collaboration and refinement.

In the next chapter, you'll take your newly crafted prompts to the next level by learning how to refine them iteratively and engage ChatGPT in dynamic, back-and-forth dialogues.

Chapter 3: Iterative Refinement and Conversational Flow

Mastering the Art of Collaboration with ChatGPT

A well-crafted prompt is a strong start, but even the best prompts can be improved through refinement. This chapter focuses on the iterative process of refining your prompts and responses to achieve the best possible outcomes. You'll learn how to engage ChatGPT in dynamic conversations, leveraging its conversational flow to clarify ideas, explore options, and uncover innovative solutions.

Through examples and exercises, we'll explore how to transform vague or general prompts into precise and actionable queries. By mastering this feedback loop, you'll gain the ability to guide ChatGPT like a true collaborator, building on its responses to achieve tailored, meaningful results.

3.1 Iterative Refinement of Prompts

The Feedback Loop

Crafting a great prompt is rarely a one-and-done process. Often, it takes a bit of back-and-forth with ChatGPT to refine your request and get the best possible response. This iterative process is known as the feedback loop—a cycle of asking, receiving, clarifying, and refining.

Think of it like collaborating with a teammate. You share your initial idea, they respond with their input, and then you refine your request based on what they provide. ChatGPT excels at this type of collaboration, making it one of its greatest strengths.

Here's an example of the feedback loop in action:

Initial Prompt

Suggest ways to market my bakery

ChatGPT's Response:

> *General ideas, such as "use social media," "host events," and "offer discounts."*

Refined Prompt

> *What are three creative, low-cost social media campaigns to promote my bakery's sourdough bread?*

ChatGPT's Response

> *Specific campaigns, such as "behind-the-scenes videos of bread-making," "weekly sourdough tips for followers," and "a photo contest for customers."*

Further Refinement

> *Can you expand on the photo contest idea? How would I run it effectively on Instagram?*

ChatGPT's Response

> *Detailed steps, including hashtags, prize ideas, and engagement tips.*

The key to the feedback loop is patience and persistence. If the initial response isn't quite what you need, don't scrap the interaction—use it as a foundation to clarify and refine your request.

The feedback loop isn't just for refining polished prompts—it's perfect for sorting through the chaos of half-formed ideas. ChatGPT can help you brainstorm, organize, and refine until you're ready to take action. We'll talk more about brainstorming with ChatGPT later in this chapter.

3.2 Steps for Refining Prompts

When refining your prompts, focus on these three areas to guide ChatGPT toward the best results:

Adding Constraints

Constraints help narrow the scope of your request, ensuring ChatGPT provides a more focused response. For example:

Suggest three social media strategies	▶	*Suggest three low-cost social media strategies to attract local customers.*

Clarifying Details

If ChatGPT's response doesn't match your needs, provide additional details or rephrase your request. For example:

Provide an overview of marketing strategies for bakeries	▶	*Explain marketing strategies that focus on social media for small bakeries.*

Improving Tone

Specify the tone you'd like ChatGPT to use to ensure the response matches your audience or purpose. For example:

Write a response to a customer complaint	▶	*Write a friendly and apologetic response to a customer complaint about a delayed shipment.*

Mastering the Feedback Loop

***Objective**: Refine prompts iteratively to achieve precise and actionable responses from ChatGPT.*

***Steps**:*

1. ***Start with a Broad Prompt**: Begin with a general idea or question to set the stage.*
   ***Example**: "Suggest marketing strategies for a bakery."*

2. ***Evaluate the Response**: Assess ChatGPT's reply for relevance, clarity, and specificity.*
   ***Ask**: Is the response actionable? Does it address your needs?*

3. ***Add Constraints to Narrow Focus**: If the response is too broad or vague, refine the prompt with specific criteria.*
   ***Example**: "Suggest three marketing strategies for a bakery targeting health-conscious customers."*

4. ***Clarify Details**: Fill in any gaps or address ambiguities in the response by adding context.*
   ***Example**: "Focus on low-cost strategies for social media engagement."*

5. ***Specify Tone or Style:** Adjust the tone or style of the output to match your preferences.*
   ***Example**: "Keep the tone friendly and conversational."*

6. ***Repeat as Necessary**: Continue refining the prompt in small steps until the response meets your expectations*
   ***Example**: "Expand on strategy #1 with an example of a social media post."*

Use this framework to guide your practice in the interactive exercises throughout this chapter and see how refining prompts step-by-step leads to better results.

3.3 Examples of Iteration in Action

To see refinement in action, let's walk through an example step-by-step:

Vague Initial Prompt

> *How do I attract more customers?*

ChatGPT's Response

> *General ideas like "advertise more," "use social media," and "offer promotions."*

Refined Prompt

> *What are three creative marketing ideas to attract local customers to a bakery?*

ChatGPT's Response

> *Specific ideas like "host a tasting event," "partner with local coffee shops," and "offer a loyalty program."*

Further Refinement

> *Can you expand on hosting a tasting event? Include ideas for themes and promotion.*

ChatGPT's Response

> *Detailed suggestions such as "seasonal tasting themes like fall flavors," "collaborations with local farms," and "using Instagram to promote the event."*

Now, let's see how the steps from the feedback loop playbook come to life with real-world examples.

Interactive Exercise

Take a vague prompt and refine it step-by-step. Start with a broad question and add constraints, clarify details, and improve the tone. Here's an example to get you started:

- ***Initial Prompt**: "How can I grow my business?"*
- ***Refined Prompt**: "What are three low-cost ways to market a small bakery?"*
- ***Further Refinement**: "What are three Instagram strategies to promote a bakery's fresh sourdough bread to health-conscious customers?"*

Write your own prompts and review how each iteration improves clarity, context, and focus.

3.4 Leveraging Conversational Flow for Collaboration

One of ChatGPT's greatest strengths is its ability to engage in dynamic, interactive conversations. Unlike search engines that provide static answers to single queries, ChatGPT enables you to collaborate through an ongoing dialogue. This conversational flow turns ChatGPT from a tool that simply retrieves information into a brainstorming partner that helps refine your ideas, solve problems, and develop strategies.

To make the most of this conversational capability, it's important to understand the distinction between transactional and conversational prompts. Transactional prompts are single, one-off queries designed to extract a specific piece of information. For example:

Prompt

What are three ways to market a bakery?

Response

ChatGPT provides useful suggestions such as, "Use social media, host events, and offer discounts."

While helpful, this type of interaction is limited to a static response and doesn't evolve further unless you initiate follow-up prompts.

Conversational prompts, on the other hand, open the door to a richer exchange of ideas. Instead of stopping at the initial suggestions, you can follow up with more specific questions, clarify your intent, or dig deeper into particular aspects of the topic. For instance:

Prompt

What are three ways to market a bakery specializing in sourdough bread?

Response

Use Instagram to share behind-the-scenes content, host a community baking class, and partner with local coffee shops.

Follow-Up Prompt

Could you expand on using social media? Which platforms should I focus on for a bakery?

Response

Focus on Instagram and TikTok for visual content. Share behind-the-scenes videos of your baking process and showcase customer testimonials.

Further Refinement

What are some free or low-cost strategies for Instagram campaigns?

Response

Create a weekly series showcasing new bread flavors, encourage customers to share photos with hashtags, and run a giveaway for free bread.

This iterative approach allows you to guide the conversation toward more tailored and actionable results, much like working with a brainstorming partner. By engaging in back-and-forth exchanges, you ensure that the output aligns with your unique needs and objectives.

Once you've mastered conversational flow, you can take it a step further by using ChatGPT as your collaborative brainstorming partner. Let's explore how to generate and refine ideas together.

3.5 Collaborative Brainstorming

The conversational flow with ChatGPT is particularly effective for tackling big-picture ideas and refining complex strategies. It's a powerful tool for helping you define your vision, clarify your goals, and develop actionable plans.

Imagine you're thinking about launching a subscription box for your bakery. You might start by asking a high-level question:

Prompt

I'm considering launching a subscription box for my bakery. What should I consider before starting?

Response

Identify your target audience, plan logistics, determine pricing, and create a marketing strategy.

Building on this response, you could refine your focus with a follow-up question:

Prompt

What could be a unique selling point for a subscription box featuring organic sourdough bread?

Response

Offer seasonal bread varieties, include exclusive recipes, or highlight locally sourced ingredients.

Finally, as you move toward execution, you could ask a more targeted question:

Prompt

How could I market this subscription box to health-conscious customers on a tight budget?

Response

Use Instagram for promotions, collaborate with local influencers, and offer referral discounts to your customers.

This process transforms a vague idea into a well-defined plan through iterative exploration and refinement.

From Vagueness to Awesomeness

Feeling stuck with a half-formed or vague idea can be frustrating, but don't worry—ChatGPT thrives on turning messy thoughts into actionable brilliance. Think of it like clearing out the junk drawer of your mind: ChatGPT's job is to organize the clutter, find the gems, and present them back to you in a neat package.

Brainstorming is about letting go of perfection. Share your rough ideas and let ChatGPT guide you toward clarity. With practice, the process becomes less awkward and more intuitive—maybe even a little fun!

You've now gained the skills to refine your prompts iteratively and engage ChatGPT in dynamic, collaborative conversations. With practice, patience, and persistence, you will be able to transform even the vaguest queries into precise, actionable insights. Leveraging conversational flow allows you to explore ideas in depth, creating a productive exchange that evolves over time.

The feedback loop playbook and exercises in this chapter are your roadmap for transforming vague prompts into actionable insights through dynamic collaboration. With these tools, you're ready to turn even the vaguest ideas into actionable insights. In the next chapter, we'll build on this collaborative approach with advanced strategies for strategic collaboration and execution.

Chapter 4: Strategic Collaboration with ChatGPT

Advanced Techniques for Turning Plans into Reality

With the foundations of crafting and refining prompts in place, it's time to elevate your interactions with ChatGPT to a strategic level. This chapter dives into advanced techniques for collaboration, including brainstorming innovative ideas, shaping long-term strategies, and executing actionable plans. You'll also discover how to navigate ChatGPT's strengths and limitations, ensuring your interactions are both productive and effective.

Whether you're developing a marketing campaign, launching a new product, or solving complex challenges, these advanced methods will empower you to maximize ChatGPT's potential as a strategic partner.

4.1 Best Practices for Collaboration

To fully leverage ChatGPT's conversational capabilities, approach your interactions as a dialogue rather than a series of isolated queries. Start with a broad question to gather initial insights, then progressively refine your focus. For example:

Prompt

What are some creative ways to market a bakery?

Response

Run a baking class, create a loyalty program, and host themed tasting events.

You could refine this further:

Follow-Up Prompt

What are some free strategies for Instagram marketing?

Response

Post behind-the-scenes content, use hashtags to engage local customers, and share customer reviews in your stories.

If a response doesn't meet your expectations, rephrasing your question can make a significant difference. For example:

Initial Prompt

Help me create a marketing plan.

Revised Prompt

Create a one-month marketing plan for a bakery specializing in organic sourdough bread.

Providing additional context or constraints often leads to more relevant and actionable responses.

Finally, collaboration benefits from treating ChatGPT as an active partner. Use conversational language to guide the exchange naturally. For example:

Your Feedback

That's a great start! Can we explore some low-cost alternatives to these strategies?

This conversational tone helps maintain a productive and engaging flow, making the interaction feel more collaborative and less transactional.

By approaching ChatGPT as a brainstorming partner and leveraging its conversational flow, you can unlock its full potential to refine ideas, overcome challenges, and develop tailored strategies that meet your goals.

4.2 ChatGPT's Strengths and Weaknesses

Understanding ChatGPT's Strengths

ChatGPT excels in areas where speed, knowledge, and flexibility are key. One of its most significant strengths is its access to a vast repository of knowledge. Whether you need to understand a complex concept, generate ideas, or explore various strategies, ChatGPT can provide quick and comprehensive responses.

Another strength is its speed in generating ideas and providing step-by-step guidance. You can go from brainstorming broad strategies to detailed execution plans in moments, saving time and effort.

ChatGPT's flexibility in tone, style, and response types is also a major asset. You can ask for formal explanations, friendly social media captions, or even creative storytelling, tailoring the output to suit your needs.

Recognizing ChatGPT's Weaknesses

While ChatGPT has become far more capable, it still isn't flawless. Modern versions can remember key details from previous sessions—such as preferences, goals, and working drafts—but this memory is optional and user-controlled. You can clear it, adjust it, or instruct the model not to store any data.

This is powerful, but it also means you shouldn't assume the AI automatically "knows everything we've already talked about." If something matters—your brand voice, your target customer, your current offer—restate it or ask the model to summarize it for reuse. That keeps the interaction aligned with your intent, rather than drifting over time.

Additionally, ChatGPT can occasionally provide inaccurate information or overlook important nuances. While its responses are often helpful, they are not always error-free or deeply analytical. For example:

Explain how to set up an email marketing campaign for a bakery.

The response would be a detailed, step-by-step guide that might overlook advanced considerations, such as legal compliance with email marketing laws in specific regions.

Ultimately, ChatGPT may struggle to understand complex nuances without highly detailed prompts. Ambiguity in your request can lead to generic or irrelevant responses.

What's the best way to grow my bakery?

The response will be general suggestions like "advertise on social media" or "offer discounts," which might not align with your specific goals.

Strategies for Leveraging Strengths

To make the most of ChatGPT's strengths, focus on areas where it excels:

Brainstorming - Use ChatGPT to generate ideas quickly. For example:

Suggest five creative ways to promote a bakery's new sourdough bread.

Research - Ask for concise explanations or overviews. For example:

What are the benefits of organic sourdough bread for health-conscious consumers?

Generating Plans - Request detailed, actionable strategies. For example:

Create a one-week content calendar for a bakery's Instagram account, focusing on seasonal bread offerings."

Recognizing ChatGPT's Weaknesses

While ChatGPT is a powerful conversational partner, it isn't perfect. One of its main limitations is that it doesn't retain memory between sessions. Each new conversation begins with a blank slate, meaning it can't recall your previous context or decisions unless you reintroduce them.

To address ChatGPT's lack of memory, you can ask it to generate a detailed prompt summarizing your old session. This summary can serve as a bridge to continue the conversation in a new session.

Can you create a detailed summary of our current discussion so I can use it to start a new session later?

In response, ChatGPT will provide a concise yet comprehensive recap of the key points and context. You can save this summary and use it as your next session's initial prompt to pick up where you left off.

I've also used this technique when I want a fresh start in a new session, especially if the current session isn't going as I hoped. I can reset the conversation with a well-crafted summary prompt while keeping it controlled and aligned with my goals.

By proactively creating summaries, you can maintain continuity across sessions or refine the flow of your interaction, ensuring that the context of your project or discussion is not lost.

Inconsistency in Tone, Style, or Approach - ChatGPT can also struggle with inconsistency in tone, style, or approach, especially during extended projects or over time or generating images. While immediate follow-up prompts requesting a similar tone often yield consistent results, longer sessions—such as developing a comprehensive marketing campaign over several hours—may result in shifts in style or tone.

This inconsistency can be disruptive when maintaining a consistent brand voice across multiple marketing materials.

While it's difficult to demonstrate this shift in a book fully, it's something you may notice during longer interactions. Pay close attention to ChatGPT's responses over time and watch for subtle tone, style, or approach changes. Recognizing these shifts early allows you to adjust or refine prompts to bring the conversation back on track.

Addressing Inconsistencies in Extended Sessions

To manage inconsistency in tasks like image generation or multi-step projects, consider the following strategies:

Clarify the Style or Theme Regularly - Whether you're crafting marketing copy or generating images, periodically check in to confirm that the output aligns with your desired style or theme. This helps course-correct any drift that may occur.

> *Can you confirm the style we've been using? It should be clean and modern with bold colors.*

Create a Detailed Reference Prompt - Once you've established a tone, style, or visual theme, ask ChatGPT to produce a detailed reference prompt. Use this as a baseline for future requests to maintain consistency.

> *Summarize the visual style and elements of the last image we created so I can ensure future images match.*

Segment Projects Into Smaller Batches - For both image generation and longer conversations, work in smaller, focused batches. After completing a segment, ask for a summary or reference that can guide the next phase of the project.

> *Summarize the tone and style we've been using for captions and provide a sample prompt I can use in a new session.*

Maintaining Image Consistency - The paid version of ChatGPT includes support for image generation, which opens up exciting possibilities for creative projects. One effective way to ensure consistency in image style is by referencing the "artistic style" directly in your prompts.

To capture the artistic style of an existing image, you can upload or reference the image and ask ChatGPT to generate a prompt that describes its style.

> *Could you write a prompt to describe the artistic style of this image? I want to use the style in future image generation requests.*

By explaining how you plan to use the generated prompt—for example, to create a series of visually cohesive images—you provide ChatGPT with valuable context, improving the quality and relevance of its output.

Using these techniques can help you maintain better control over consistency, even for complex or extended projects. As with other tasks, it's important to watch for subtle shifts in tone, style, or visual elements and take proactive steps to address them as needed.

4.3 Advanced Techniques for Shaping Strategy

Crafting strategic prompts is one of the most valuable ways to leverage ChatGPT. Whether you're envisioning a high-level plan or diving into execution details, ChatGPT can serve as a collaborative partner, helping you develop, refine, and execute your ideas. This section explores advanced techniques to take your interactions to the next level.

From Prompt Engineering to Prompt Strategy

The focus has shifted from crafting one-off "perfect" prompts to building repeatable **prompt strategies**. A prompt strategy is a structured, reusable process for thinking through a problem — not just typing clever phrasing.

A solid strategy involves five elements:

1. **Define the role and intent** — Clarify who the model should act as and what outcome you expect.

2. **Provide context and examples** — Include artifacts such as style guides, tone notes, or data snippets.

3. **Constrain the output** — Specify structure, length, or schema.

4. **Iterate with refinement** — Move from high-level vision to tactical execution.

5. **Ground with checks** — Add test cases or ask for critiques to validate accuracy.

Treat this as a strategic conversation — one where you guide the model through reasoning, verification, and iteration to reach results that consistently align with your goals.

High-Level Vision Prompts - These prompts focus on overarching goals, opportunities, or challenges. They help you define the "what" and "why" of your strategy, offering clarity on your big-picture objectives.

> *I want to expand my bakery to include a subscription box service. What factors should I consider when building a successful subscription model for health-conscious customers?*

Execution-Focused Prompts - These prompts delve into the "how" of achieving your goals, turning vision into actionable steps. They're designed to focus on specific tasks or processes.

> *Create a step-by-step plan for launching a subscription box service for a bakery specializing in organic sourdough bread.*

By combining both high-level vision and execution-focused prompts, you can maintain a clear strategic direction while laying out a practical path forward.

Evolving Ideas Over Time

Big-picture questions often require breaking down into smaller, manageable discussions. ChatGPT's conversational nature makes it ideal for iterative refinement, allowing you to evolve your ideas through dialogue.

Start with a broad question to establish a foundation, then progressively narrow the focus to explore specific aspects.

Initial Prompt

> *What are some creative ways to market a bakery to health-conscious customers?*

Follow-Up Prompt

> *Can we focus on free or low-cost marketing strategies?*

Further Refinement

> *What would a detailed content calendar look like for promoting organic sourdough bread on Instagram?*

This approach allows you to dig deeper into each element of your strategy, uncovering insights and refining your plan one step at a time.

Practical Execution

Once you've brainstormed and refined your strategy, it's time to turn ideas into action. ChatGPT can help you develop concrete execution plans tailored to your specific needs.

> *Draft a one-month marketing plan to promote a bakery's subscription box for organic sourdough bread. Include social media campaigns, email outreach, and in-store promotions.*

ChatGPT can also assist with tactical details, such as crafting social media posts, designing email templates, or creating event checklists. By shifting from high-level vision to granular execution, you can ensure your strategy is actionable and results-driven.

Interactive Exercise

Practice using advanced techniques to shape strategy by crafting a series of prompts:

Start with a vision-level prompt:

- ***Prompt**: "What are the key factors to consider when creating a brand for a bakery specializing in organic sourdough bread?"*
- ***Transition** into tactical execution prompts:*
  - ***Prompt**: "Based on a health-conscious brand identity, what would be three key messages to highlight in marketing materials?"*
  - ***Follow-Up Prompt**: "Create a step-by-step plan for launching a brand awareness campaign for this bakery."*

Compare the results and analyze how each type of prompt contributes to shaping your overall strategy. Reflect on how evolving from a broad vision to tactical execution can provide clarity and structure to your projects.

4.4 Putting It All Together

Now that you've explored the foundational principles and advanced techniques for working with ChatGPT, it's time to see how everything fits together in a cohesive workflow. This section walks you through a comprehensive example, showcasing how to lead a project from vision to execution using the methods you've learned. We'll also provide a handy checklist to guide you in applying these strategies effectively in your own projects.

Leading Strategic Collaboration with ChatGPT

***Objective**: Effectively collaborate with ChatGPT to brainstorm, refine, and execute strategic ideas for your business.*

***Steps**:*

1. ***Define Your Project's Vision and Goals**: Start by identifying the purpose of your project. What are you trying to achieve? Be specific about the outcome you're aiming for.*
   ***Example**: "I want to create a marketing plan for a bakery to increase sales during the holiday season."*

2. ***Craft a High-Level Prompt**: Write a broad initial prompt to start the brainstorming process. Use this to set the stage and explore general ideas.*
   ***Example**: "What are some effective holiday marketing strategies for a bakery specializing in organic goods?"*

3. ***Use Iterative Refinement**: Refine the response step-by-step by adding constraints, clarifying details, and narrowing the focus.*
   ***Example Refinement**:*
   - ***Add Constraints**: "Focus on low-cost strategies."*
   - ***Clarify Details**: "Target families shopping for holiday gifts."*

4. ***Transition to Tactical Prompts**: Once you have a clear strategy, break it into smaller, actionable tasks with specific prompts.*
   ***Example**:*
   - *"Create a one-week social media calendar featuring holiday-themed posts."*
   - *"Draft email copy for a holiday promotion."*

5. ***Summarize and Reintroduce Context**: Summarize the progress so far and reintroduce the context if needed to maintain continuity.*
   ***Example**: "So far, we've planned a social media calendar and an email campaign. Let's focus next on in-store promotions for the holiday season."*

6. ***Evaluate and Adjust**: Review the output generated. Are they aligned with your goals? Adjust prompts or reframe questions as needed to improve results.*
   ***Example**: "These email ideas are too formal. Can you make them more casual and family-friendly?"*

Tips for Success

- **Be Patient**: Strategic collaboration is a process—allow time for iteration.
- **Stay Flexible**: Adjust your prompts based on the outputs to guide the conversation effectively.
- **Focus on Outcomes**: Keep the end goal in mind to stay on track.

Comprehensive Example: Launching an Online Subscription Service

Imagine you're running an online business that offers a subscription service for personalized meal plans. Let's follow this project step-by-step, applying the techniques covered in this chapter.

Defining Vision and Goals - Start by setting the overall direction for the project.

I want to launch a subscription service for personalized meal plans targeting busy professionals. What are the key factors to consider when building a successful subscription model?

The response outlines considerations like understanding the target audience, defining the personalization process, planning logistics, setting pricing tiers, and creating a marketing strategy.

Exploring Strategic Vision - Delve deeper into the unique aspects of your subscription service.

What could be a unique selling point for a personalized meal plan subscription targeting busy professionals?

The response will provide ideas such as quick preparation times, customizable dietary preferences, integration with grocery delivery apps, and exclusive access to professional nutrition advice, which will emerge as potential differentiators.

Crafting Clear, Structured Prompts - Transition from vision to execution by requesting specific plans.

> *Create a step-by-step plan for launching this subscription service, including customer onboarding, marketing, and logistics.*

In response, ChatGPT generates a roadmap covering initial setup, targeted advertising, customer retention strategies, and operational workflows.

Review the response and refine it for greater precision.

Prompt

> *Suggest some marketing strategies for the subscription service.*

Example Follow-Up Prompt

> *Focus on email marketing strategies for onboarding and retaining customers, with examples of subject lines and calls to action.*

ChatGPT will deliver a refined response that delivers tailored email campaign ideas, such as a welcome series for new subscribers, personalized recipe suggestions, and renewal reminders with incentives.

Using Conversational Flow for Collaboration - Build on ChatGPT's suggestions through iterative conversations.

> *Expand on the idea of grocery delivery integration. How can I communicate this feature effectively to potential customers?*

In response, ChatGPT suggests messaging like "Save time with meal plans delivered to your door" and creating partnerships with popular grocery apps for seamless user experiences.

Leveraging Strengths and Compensating for Weaknesses - Ensure consistency and accuracy by addressing potential weaknesses.

> *Summarize all the marketing strategies we've discussed so far and create a prompt I can use in a new session to maintain continuity.*

In response, ChatGPT will generate a detailed summary and reusable prompt, ensuring future conversations align with your project's established tone and strategy.

Practical Execution - Finally, translate the refined plan into actionable steps.

Create a one-month email marketing calendar for the subscription service, including topics, subject lines, and goals for each campaign.

In response, ChatGPT provides a detailed schedule, such as onboarding emails during the first week, tips for quick meal prep in the second week, and testimonials from satisfied customers in the third week to build trust.

By following this structured approach, you can lead ChatGPT through every phase of a project, from brainstorming to actionable outcomes, ensuring clarity and alignment throughout.

4.5 Checklist for Leading with ChatGPT

Use this checklist to guide your interactions with ChatGPT and ensure a streamlined, effective process:

- **Define Vision and Goals** - Clearly articulate the purpose and objectives of your project.
- **Craft Clear, Structured Prompts** - Provide context, specify tasks, and include tone or style as needed.
- **Refine Through Iteration** - Review responses and adjust prompts to clarify or narrow the focus.
- **Use Conversational Flow and Collaboration** - Build on ChatGPT's responses through iterative, back-and-forth exchanges.
- **Leverage Strengths and Compensate for Weaknesses** - Take advantage of ChatGPT's speed and flexibility while addressing its limitations by reintroducing context or validating information.
- **Summarize and Reintroduce Context for Continuity** - Use summaries or reference prompts to maintain consistency across sessions, especially for long-term projects.

This comprehensive process ensures that you can harness ChatGPT as a valuable partner in achieving your project goals.

4.6 Summary

In this chapter, you've explored advanced techniques for working with ChatGPT, including strategic brainstorming, refining long-term plans, and overcoming its limitations. By applying these methods, you can harness ChatGPT's capabilities to tackle complex challenges and execute actionable strategies with confidence.

Next, we'll shift our focus to generating innovative business ideas. You'll learn how to spark creativity, identify new opportunities, and transform abstract concepts into practical plans. Get ready to explore how ChatGPT can fuel your entrepreneurial vision!

Chapter 5: Innovate with ChatGPT: Generating Business Ideas

Unleash Creativity, Identify Trends, and Validate Your Vision

Imagine having a brainstorming partner who never tires, brings fresh perspectives, and has access to vast industry knowledge. ChatGPT can serve as exactly that—a powerful tool to spark creativity, identify market opportunities, and transform rough concepts into actionable business ideas.

In this chapter, you'll discover how to leverage ChatGPT to brainstorm innovative ideas, explore market trends, and refine your concepts into practical, validated business opportunities. Whether you're pursuing a side hustle or launching your next big venture, ChatGPT's AI-powered creativity will help you navigate the path from inspiration to execution.

5.1 Using ChatGPT for Brainstorming

The first step in business ideation is often a brainstorming session, where you generate a wide range of ideas to explore. ChatGPT can help you think beyond the obvious by suggesting fresh perspectives, unexpected niches, and unique twists on existing concepts.

Embracing Every Idea, Even the "Bad" Ones

When I was in middle school, a teacher taught us an invaluable lesson: never disregard a "bad" idea when brainstorming. The reasoning behind this was simple yet profound—sometimes, it's those seemingly unusable ideas that spark the truly great ones. Decades later, after countless brainstorming sessions, I've found this advice to be true again and again. Exploring every thought, even those that seem outlandish, can lead to unexpected insights or inspire better ideas you might not reach otherwise.

With ChatGPT, this approach becomes even more effective. ChatGPT has a knack for generating ideas that range from the practical to the wildly imaginative. Rather than filtering out the less appealing ones immediately, consider how each suggestion might be adapted, combined, or inspire something new.

Idea Generation Prompts

To begin, try using ChatGPT to generate a variety of business ideas tailored to specific industries, investment levels, or personal skills. Here are some prompts to help you get started:

Prompts

Generate unique business ideas in the [industry type] sector.
What are some trending business ideas in [year] that require minimal investment?
Suggest business ideas for someone skilled in [specific skill or industry].

Each of these prompts opens up different possibilities, pushing ChatGPT to think creatively based on your specified interests or industry focus. Experiment with variations to expand the pool of ideas further.

Expanding on Existing Ideas

If you already have a rough business concept in mind, ChatGPT can help refine and expand it. Ask for features, variations, or enhancements tailored to specific target audiences:

Prompts

How could I expand a digital marketing consultancy to cater to small businesses?
What are some additional revenue streams for a subscription box service?
Suggest some unique features to make a mobile app for language learning stand out.

With these kinds of prompts, ChatGPT can help transform a basic concept into a well-rounded business idea, suggesting elements that add depth and differentiate it from competitors.

5.2 Exploring Market Gaps and Trends

Finding gaps in the market or identifying emerging trends can lead to lucrative business opportunities. ChatGPT can support your exploration by simulating market research and providing insights into underserved areas.

Market Research with ChatGPT

ChatGPT can be your initial research assistant, helping you explore broad market gaps or customer pain points within an industry. Try prompts like:

Prompts

Identify common pain points in the [industry] sector that a new business could address.
What customer needs are currently underserved in [specific market]?
List recent trends in [industry] and how a new business could capitalize on them.

Using ChatGPT to perform this initial research, you can gain insights into potential areas for differentiation and innovation, laying the groundwork for ideas catering to specific, unaddressed needs.

Competitive Analysis

Understanding the competitive landscape is crucial for developing a distinctive business concept. Use ChatGPT to gather general competitive insights and explore ways to stand out:

Prompts

Who are the main competitors in [specific industry] and what are their strengths?
What gaps do existing businesses in [industry] often overlook?
Suggest ways for a [type of business] to differentiate itself in a crowded market.

Through these prompts, ChatGPT can help you identify positioning strategies and unique value propositions that set your business apart.

Bad Ideas Are Bridges to Good Ones

Sometimes, the fastest path to a great idea is through a bunch of bad ones. Don't be afraid to let ChatGPT help you brainstorm the wild, wacky, or impractical. Each idea you generate sharpens your focus and gets you closer to the winner.

5.3 Understanding and Defining Your Customer

To succeed in any business, understanding your customer isn't just helpful—it's essential. The more deeply you know who your customers are, the better you can meet their needs, solve their problems, and create products or services they genuinely value. In this section, we'll explore how to use ChatGPT to build a clear picture of your target audience and develop insights that can guide your marketing, product development, and customer engagement strategies.

Starting with a Broad Customer Profile

Think of your customer profile as a sketch of who you believe your target audience is. This initial profile can be based on what you know, observed, or even industry trends. Start by feeding ChatGPT basic details about your business and product, such as the industry, your core offerings, and any assumptions you already have about your audience. For example:

> *I own a local coffee shop that emphasizes sustainability and sources beans from small farms. I think my customers are environmentally conscious and prefer quality over quantity. Can you help me outline a profile of my ideal customer?*

ChatGPT can use this information to help you create a high-level profile that touches on demographics, interests, and values. This profile provides a starting point for further exploration and refinement, opening the door to a greater understanding of your audience.

Exploring Customer Pain Points

Once you have a general idea of your audience, dig deeper into their pain points. Understanding their challenges or problems helps you position your product as a solution. For instance, if you run an online fitness service, consider the common barriers people experience in maintaining a fitness routine, such as lack of motivation or time.

> *My online fitness service targets people with busy schedules. Can you help me list some challenges they might face when trying to stay fit?*

Based on ChatGPT's response, you can start crafting your messaging and product features around these pain points. This exercise helps refine your understanding of the customer and identifies specific needs that your product can address, allowing you to align your offerings more closely with what matters to them.

Building Detailed Customer Personas

A persona takes the high-level profile and pain points further by creating a more nuanced, personal snapshot of a "typical" customer. Personas are fictional characters representing your target customers, complete with names, backgrounds, and preferences. ChatGPT can help you build these personas by combining the information gathered in earlier steps.

Based on my coffee shop's focus on sustainability and quality, can you help me create a detailed customer persona for someone who would frequently visit my shop?

ChatGPT may provide you with a persona like "Samantha, a 28-year-old freelance designer who values eco-friendly brands and enjoys supporting local businesses." You can then refine or create multiple personas, each representing different customer segments that your business may attract. These personas guide not only your marketing but also how you design and deliver your products, ensuring they resonate with real people's lives.

Using ChatGPT to Segment Your Audience

Once you have a clear picture of your general audience and specific personas, consider how your audience might break down into different segments. Segmentation helps you target more precisely and tailor your messaging and offerings to each group. ChatGPT can assist by identifying potential segments based on different needs, preferences, or behaviors.

Can you suggest ways to segment my audience for a sustainable coffee shop? I want to reach both regular daily customers and occasional specialty buyers.

ChatGPT can help you create distinctions between segments, like "everyday eco-conscious drinkers" versus "weekend specialty buyers," so that you can customize your strategies for each. Perhaps your daily regulars appreciate loyalty discounts, while your specialty buyers respond more to exclusive, small-batch offers. This tailored approach enhances customer satisfaction and retention, as each segment feels like your business truly "gets" them.

Gauging Customer Sentiment

Understanding how your customers feel about your product or service can provide invaluable insights into their experience and loyalty. You can use ChatGPT to analyze customer feedback from reviews, social media comments, or survey responses, helping you identify trends and adjust accordingly.

Based on these customer reviews, can you help me analyze the sentiment and identify any common positive or negative themes?

Providing ChatGPT with actual feedback snippets allows it to highlight trends, such as consistent praise for the coffee quality or recurring complaints about wait times. This kind of analysis reveals strengths you can emphasize and weaknesses you can address to improve customer satisfaction.

Continuous Improvement Through Customer Feedback

Customer needs and preferences evolve, and your understanding of them should, too. Regularly revisiting your customer profile, pain points, and personas ensures you stay aligned with your audience as they grow and change. ChatGPT can serve as a valuable tool in this continuous improvement process, helping you refresh and refine your understanding over time.

It's been a year since we launched our sustainable coffee line. Can you help me review our target audience and suggest any updates based on new trends in the industry?

This proactive approach enables your business to stay agile and responsive, keeping you ahead of trends and attuned to your audience's shifting needs. ChatGPT helps make this ongoing process more manageable by offering a fresh perspective on your evolving customer landscape.

Don't Overthink It—Prototype It!

Your first idea doesn't have to be perfect. Use ChatGPT to create a quick prototype, test it, and learn from the results. Iteration is where innovation happens—don't let perfectionism slow you down!

Think Like a Detective!

Every business idea starts with a mystery: What do customers need? What's missing in the market? Use ChatGPT to uncover trends, identify gaps, and gather insights—like a business detective solving a case.

After identifying a promising business idea, validating it before committing resources can save time and reduce risks. ChatGPT can help simulate early feedback, offering insights into potential challenges and customer responses.

Assessing Feasibility

Use ChatGPT to evaluate the practicality of your ideas by considering startup costs, scalability, and required resources. Some prompts to get you started including:

Prompts

What are some potential barriers to starting a [type of business]?
What resources would be essential for launching an online course platform?
Suggest ways to make a small-scale food delivery service more scalable."

Through these queries, ChatGPT can help you anticipate obstacles, assess required investments, and adjust plans accordingly.

Early Feedback Simulation

Although ChatGPT can't directly connect you with customers, it can help simulate how potential customers might respond to your idea. For example:

What might a target customer say about a [specific product/service] aimed at [audience]?
List possible customer feedback points for a subscription box focused on eco-friendly products.
Identify common objections customers might have to a freelance web design business.

By identifying potential responses early, you can refine your offering and address concerns before launch.

Feedback Is a Superpower!

Validating your idea is like having a conversation with your future customers. Use ChatGPT to simulate feedback and refine your ideas before bringing them to the real world. The more feedback you seek, the better your outcomes will be.

From Brainstorm to Business Plan

Objective: *Guide readers through the process of brainstorming, refining, and validating business ideas to create a clear and actionable business plan.*

Steps:

1. ***Brainstorm Broad Ideas***: *Use ChatGPT to explore a variety of potential business ideas based on your skills, interests, or market trends.*
   Example: *"Suggest ten business ideas for someone skilled in graphic design."*

2. ***Explore Market Gaps and Trends***: *Research unmet needs or emerging trends that align with your skills or target industry.*
   Example: *"What are some underserved markets in the graphic design industry?"*

3. ***Refine and Focus***: *Narrow down your ideas by defining target customers, pain points, and potential solutions.*
   Example: *"For a graphic design business targeting small businesses, what common pain points could I address?"*

4. ***Validate the Idea***: *Test the feasibility of your idea by simulating customer feedback and exploring potential challenges.*
   Example: *"Act as a small business owner. What concerns would you have about hiring a graphic designer?"*

   Use ChatGPT to outline a simple SWOT analysis (Strengths, Weaknesses, Opportunities, Threats).

5. ***Draft a Quick Business Plan Outline***: *Create a high-level business plan including your value proposition, target audience, marketing strategies, and revenue model.*
   Example: *"Help me draft a one-page business plan for a graphic design service targeting small businesses."*

6. ***Iterate and Improve***: *Refine the plan based on additional feedback or insights. Break down larger sections (e.g., marketing) into more detailed prompts for deeper exploration.*
   Example: *"Suggest three creative, low-cost marketing strategies for a new graphic design service."*

Tips for Success:

- **Think Big, Start Small**: Begin with broad ideas and refine them step-by-step to keep the process manageable.
- **Stay Open to Iteration**: Treat feedback as an opportunity to improve, not as a setback.
- **Focus on Your Strengths**: Align ideas with what you know and excel at, leveraging your unique expertise.

5.5 Generate a Quick Business Plan Outline

Once an idea is validated, creating a business plan can clarify your strategy and set goals for growth. ChatGPT can assist with drafting an initial outline, providing a high-level structure for your business plan.

High-Level Business Plan Components

Use ChatGPT to outline major sections of a business plan, ensuring that you cover essential aspects like mission, vision, and revenue models:

Create a basic outline for a business plan for a [specific type of business].

What should be included in a business plan for a subscription service?

Draft a mission and vision statement for a [type of business].

With these structured prompts, ChatGPT can help you build a business plan skeleton that you can later flesh out with specifics.

Setting Short-Term and Long-Term Goals

Setting clear goals can give your business a strong foundation. ChatGPT can help by generating achievable short- and long-term milestones:

Suggest initial goals for a small online retail business.

What are some long-term objectives for a business in [industry]?

These goals provide direction and make it easier to track progress, adapt, and grow in the early stages of your business.

Interactive Challenge

Ready to take your business ideas to the next level? Try this three-step challenge with ChatGPT:

- ***Generate Ideas**: Ask ChatGPT for 10 unique business ideas in your chosen industry.*
- ***Evaluate Feasibility**: Select three ideas and explore their practicality by asking about costs, audience, and required resources.*
- ***Refine One Idea**: Choose your favorite and dive deeper—ask ChatGPT how to make it stand out or appeal to a specific audience.*

By completing this challenge, you'll experience firsthand how ChatGPT can transform a simple idea into an actionable business concept.

5.6 Summary

This chapter showed how ChatGPT can be your ultimate partner in business ideation, helping you brainstorm innovative ideas, uncover market gaps, and define your target audience. By using ChatGPT to explore trends, validate concepts, and outline quick business plans, you can move forward with clarity and confidence.

With the techniques covered in this chapter, ChatGPT becomes more than a tool—it's a creative and strategic collaborator, guiding you from the spark of an idea to actionable plans. Whether you're seeking inspiration or fine-tuning a business concept, ChatGPT can help you take your vision to the next level.

Chapter 6: Mastering Market Validation with AI

From Consumer Insights to Data-Driven Decisions

In today's fast-paced markets, making the right decisions often hinges on your ability to understand trends, predict customer behavior, and validate your ideas with precision. This is where AI steps in—not just as a tool, but as a game-changing partner that turns complex data into clear, actionable insights.

This chapter dives into how AI can revolutionize market validation. You'll learn how to use predictive analytics to forecast trends, sentiment analysis to gauge public opinion, and competitor insights to stay ahead of the curve. Whether you're fine-tuning a product or launching something entirely new, these techniques will empower you to make confident, data-driven decisions.

6.1 Techniques for AI Market Validation

When it comes to market analysis, modern tools like **Google Looker Studio** or **Power BI** are like helpful guides who can quickly show you patterns and trends hiding within your data. Predictive analytics relies on historical data to forecast future outcomes, enabling you to make informed decisions instead of relying on guesswork. These tools make the process intuitive, helping you visualize trends and anticipate shifts in consumer behavior. It's like having a weather forecast for your business, ensuring you're prepared for both sunny skies and rainy days.

Data is Your Crystal Ball

Think of AI as your business fortune-teller. It won't predict everything, but with the right data, it'll show you trends, opportunities, and risks hiding in plain sight.

Leveraging Sentiment Analysis

Imagine having a way to gauge public opinion at scale, reading emotions hidden in online conversations, reviews, and feedback. That's the power of sentiment analysis tools like **Brandwatch** or **Sprout Social**. These platforms help you track whether customers are loving, criticizing, or feeling neutral about your brand. By organizing sentiments into actionable categories, you can respond more effectively—tweaking your strategies to amplify positive experiences or address concerns in real-time. Think of it as your personal radar for customer emotions, keeping you in sync with your audience's evolving perceptions.

Simplified Data Collection

Data collection often feels like trying to piece together a jigsaw puzzle without a guide. Tools like **Browse AI** simplify this by gathering and organizing data from across the web without requiring technical expertise. Whether it's monitoring social media for trends or extracting key information from competitor websites, these platforms act like a virtual assistant, delivering only the most relevant pieces of the puzzle. Additionally, **Google Trends** provides insights into search behavior, helping you understand what's capturing people's attention. These tools are your map to uncovering valuable insights that can shape your market strategy.

Machine Learning for Trend Prediction

Once your data is collected, tools like **Google Sheets Forecasting Add-ons** or **Excel** help you identify patterns and predict future trends. These accessible platforms use algorithms to uncover shifts in consumer demand or spot anomalies that might signal emerging opportunities. It's like having a detective who sifts through the data to reveal where the market is headed. For businesses looking to stay ahead, these predictive tools offer clarity and confidence in planning your next move.

Accessible Competitor Analysis

Understanding your competition doesn't require a high-tech command center. Tools like **SEMrush** or **Google Trends** allow you to analyze what competitors are doing and identify gaps you can fill. From keyword analysis to social media strategies, these platforms help you spot opportunities to differentiate your business. Think of it as having binoculars into your competitors' strategies, empowering you to stay one step ahead and lead the market rather than follow it.

6.2 The Impact of AI-Driven Market Validation

AI-powered tools are transforming how businesses understand and engage with their markets. Whether it's visualizing trends, gauging customer sentiment, or predicting demand, these technologies empower you to turn data into actionable insights. By leveraging accessible tools for market validation, you can make confident, data-driven decisions and adapt to changes faster than ever before. In today's competitive landscape, AI isn't just a tool—it's your business ally, helping you thrive with every calculated step.

By completing this exercise, you'll gain hands-on experience with AI-powered market validation, turning abstract concepts into actionable results.

Validating Your Market with AI

Objective: *Guide readers through using AI for market validation, from data collection to actionable insights.*

Steps:

1. ***Identify*** *your market validation goal.*
2. ***Choose*** *AI tools for sentiment analysis, competitor insights, or trend forecasting.*
3. ***Analyze*** *data and validate findings using AI-driven A/B testing.*
4. ***Implement*** *adjustments based on feedback and insights.*
5. ***Repeat*** *as needed for continuous improvement.*

6.3 Leveraging AI for Consumer Insights

Understanding your customers has always been at the heart of successful businesses. AI now makes this process faster, more precise, and incredibly insightful. From decoding customer emotions to predicting future trends, AI can provide the data-driven insights needed to adapt your strategies, personalize your offerings, and stay ahead of the competition.

Real-Time Emotion Detection on Social Media

Social media is a treasure trove of unfiltered consumer sentiment. AI tools like **Sprout Social** and **Brandwatch** analyze these posts in real time, identifying emotional cues within customer comments and reviews. Whether someone's raving about your product or sharing frustrations, emotion detection helps you gauge the overall mood of your audience.

This real-time awareness enables businesses to act swiftly—resolving negative feedback before it escalates or amplifying positive sentiment to strengthen customer loyalty. Think of it as having a digital pulse on the emotions driving customer engagement, helping you foster stronger, more meaningful connections.

Tracking and Analyzing Behavior Patterns

AI doesn't just stop at emotions; it delves deep into the "what" and "why" of customer actions. Tools like **Google Analytics** and **Shopify Reports** can track consumer behavior across platforms, revealing purchase patterns and habits. For example, you might notice that customers who buy a particular product tend to pair it with another. This is where **basket analysis** comes in—helping you identify complementary products to bundle or cross-promote.

AI's ability to track and analyze behavior means you can refine your marketing and inventory strategies, ensuring you're delivering exactly what customers want, when they want it.

Building Detailed Customer Segments

Knowing your customers as individuals is key, but understanding them as groups takes it a step further. AI-driven segmentation tools like **HubSpot** or **Zoho CRM** divide your audience into meaningful categories based on shared behaviors, demographics, or preferences.

For example, AI might help you identify "frequent buyers of eco-friendly products" versus "occasional shoppers looking for seasonal deals." This segmentation enables you to target each group with tailored messaging, increasing the likelihood of engagement and conversions. Instead of speaking broadly to all customers, you can craft campaigns that resonate deeply with specific segments, ensuring your efforts hit the mark every time.

Predicting Consumer Needs and Trends

One of AI's most transformative applications is its ability to forecast future consumer needs. Tools like **Google Trends** or **Microsoft Power BI** analyze historical data to predict what products or services will be in demand. Whether it's preparing for a seasonal spike in sales or identifying an emerging trend before your competitors, predictive analytics helps you anticipate and meet customer expectations.

By leveraging AI models for demand forecasting, you avoid overstocking or understocking, ensuring your resources are allocated efficiently. Additionally, AI trend identification allows you to innovate strategically, aligning your offerings with the next big market opportunity.

Exploring Consumer Insights

Take a moment to reflect on your audience and consider the following:

- ***Patterns and Behaviors**: What patterns or behaviors would you like to understand better? For example: Why do customers abandon their shopping carts, or what motivates repeat purchases?*
- ***Customer Feedback**: What emotional responses do you want to explore in customer feedback?*
- ***Reviews**: Consider analyzing common themes in positive and negative reviews.*
- ***Segmentation**: How could segmentation improve your outreach?*
- ***Targeted Campaigns**: Think about how targeted campaigns might resonate with specific groups of customers.*

Use these questions to define areas where AI-powered insights could make the biggest difference. Then, set up a small test using tools mentioned in this chapter to begin uncovering actionable insights.

6.4 Testing and Iterating with AI Feedback

Iterative testing and refinement are essential for creating successful products and strategies. AI tools make this process faster, smarter, and more precise by automating A/B testing, refining feedback loops, and accelerating prototyping. These capabilities allow you to experiment, learn, and improve continuously.

AI-Driven A/B Testing: Data-Driven Decisions Made Easy

A/B testing helps businesses compare different variations of a product feature, webpage, or marketing strategy to determine which performs better. With AI, this process becomes streamlined and data-driven. Tools like **Optimizely**, **VWO**, or **Convert** to automate test creation, monitor real-time performance, and provide actionable insights.

For example, AI can help you test two email subject lines to see which generates higher open rates or evaluate different landing page designs to identify which converts more visitors into customers. Real-time analytics offer clear, measurable results, ensuring that decisions are guided by data, not guesswork. This precision eliminates unnecessary risk and keeps your strategies evolving effectively.

Refining Offerings Through Continuous Feedback Loops

Gathering insights from A/B testing is only the beginning. AI tools like **Qualtrics** or **SurveyMonkey** can create dynamic feedback loops, capturing user responses and preferences to help refine your product or service. Feedback loops ensure that customer input isn't just collected—it's used to drive continuous improvement.

For instance, after launching a product, you can use AI to analyze customer reviews, survey responses, or in-app behavior. AI will highlight specific areas where adjustments are needed, such as simplifying a feature or enhancing design elements. This iterative process keeps your offerings aligned with customer expectations, turning small improvements into significant gains over time.

Accelerating Prototyping with AI Tools

Prototyping often feels like a bottleneck in innovation. AI-assisted design tools like **Figma** or **Canva** help speed up the process, enabling you to iterate quickly without compromising quality. These platforms allow you to visualize and test ideas before full-scale production, saving both time and resources.

Additionally, virtual simulations powered by AI offer a risk-free testing environment. For example, you can simulate a new feature's performance or customer interaction to identify potential issues before deployment.

This not only reduces costs but also encourages experimentation, allowing you to test bold ideas without fear of failure.

Measuring Success with AI-Backed Metrics

Metrics are critical for understanding whether your efforts are succeeding. AI tools like **Google Analytics** or **HubSpot** provide powerful insights into key performance indicators (KPIs) such as:

- **Conversion Rates**: Track how effectively your website or campaign turns visitors into paying customers.
- **Customer Satisfaction**: Use survey results or review analysis to measure how well your product meets user expectations.
- **Retention Rates**: Identify how many customers return and understand what keeps them engaged.

These metrics help paint a clear picture of what's working and what needs improvement. By combining these insights with AI's rapid analysis, you can make data-informed adjustments that drive growth and satisfaction.

Staying Ahead with Rapid Iteration and AI Guidance

AI empowers businesses to iterate faster and smarter. Whether refining a product feature, improving a marketing strategy, or testing a new service, AI's ability to process data and provide actionable insights allows you to adapt quickly to market demands. This isn't just about keeping up; it's about staying ahead.

By embracing AI for testing and feedback, you ensure that your business remains agile, innovative, and aligned with customer needs in an ever-evolving marketplace.

6.5 Aligning AI Solutions with Market Needs

To succeed in today's competitive landscape, AI solutions must be more than just advanced—they need to align seamlessly with your specific market needs. Customizing AI tools, fostering continuous learning, and balancing innovation with demand ensures your business stays relevant and effective.

Customizing AI for Targeted Market Fit

AI is not a one-size-fits-all solution. Tailoring it to fit your business and audience is critical for maximizing its potential. This involves adapting AI to regional, cultural, and industry-specific requirements.

- **Localization of AI Solutions**: Localization goes beyond language translation. It involves understanding regional preferences, cultural nuances, and regulatory requirements. For example, AI solutions in retail might need to accommodate local buying habits or customer service expectations. Tools like **DeepL for translations** or **Zoho Desk** with multilingual support can help businesses cater to diverse audiences.

- **Industry-Specific Adaptations**: Different industries have unique needs, and AI tools must address them accordingly. In healthcare, AI might focus on patient diagnostics and privacy compliance, while in retail, it emphasizes inventory optimization and personalized recommendations. Customizing AI applications ensures they deliver the most value for your specific sector.

Embracing Continuous Learning and Adaptation

Markets evolve rapidly, and your AI systems must keep pace. By integrating adaptive algorithms and fostering continuous data input, businesses can ensure their AI solutions remain relevant and effective.

- **Adaptive Algorithms and Continuous Data Input**: AI systems thrive on fresh data. Continuous updates allow your AI to adapt to shifting market trends, consumer behaviors, and emerging challenges. Tools like **Microsoft Power BI** or **Tableau** can process and integrate real-time data, helping your AI systems stay in tune with the market.

- **Feedback-Driven AI Training**: Customer feedback is a valuable resource for refining AI models. Whether through surveys, product reviews, or user behavior analysis, feedback loops help ensure AI systems meet real-world needs. For example, an e-commerce platform could use customer reviews to improve its product recommendation engine.

Integrating Customer Feedback into AI Development

Building AI systems that truly meet user needs requires integrating customer insights into every stage of development. This approach ensures AI remains user-centered and responsive.

- **User-Centered Development Cycles**: Regularly revisiting AI functionality based on customer feedback helps fine-tune its performance. For instance, if users report frustration with a chatbot's tone, adjustments can be made to improve its conversational style. Incorporating feedback ensures your AI evolves alongside customer expectations.

- **Proactive Feedback Collection**: Use tools like **Qualtrics** or **SurveyMonkey** to gather structured insights. Regularly analyzing this data ensures your AI remains aligned with changing user preferences and requirements.

Balancing Innovation with Market Demand

Innovating without market alignment risks wasting time and resources. Successful businesses balance cutting-edge developments with customer expectations.

- **Strategic Innovation Roadmaps**: These roadmaps guide AI innovation efforts, ensuring new features or updates directly address customer needs. For instance, introducing an AI-powered loyalty program in retail could stem from customer demand for personalized rewards.

- **Market-Driven Pivots**: AI enables businesses to pivot quickly when market conditions change. For example, during sudden demand spikes for specific products, AI can optimize supply chains or shift marketing strategies in real-time. Balancing innovation with actionable data ensures your business remains agile and relevant.

AI as an Adaptive Business Partner

By aligning AI solutions with market needs, businesses can transform AI from a tool into a strategic partner. Customization, continuous learning, and customer feedback ensure that your AI systems remain effective, responsive, and ready to tackle future challenges. Balancing innovation with real-world demands allows you to lead with purpose and confidence in an ever-evolving marketplace.

6.6 Summary

In this chapter, we explored how AI transforms market validation into a strategic advantage. From predictive analytics and sentiment analysis to competitor research and trend forecasting, AI equips you with tools to make smarter, data-driven decisions. By leveraging AI's capabilities, you can identify underserved markets, understand customer behavior, and refine your business strategies with precision.

But data and insights are just the beginning. To fully capitalize on these market opportunities, you need an operational foundation that supports seamless execution and unparalleled efficiency. In the next chapter, we'll dive into how AI can revolutionize your daily operations—automating tasks, enhancing productivity, and ensuring your business runs like a well-oiled machine. Ready to streamline your workflows and reclaim your time? Let's get to work!

Chapter 7: AI-Powered Productivity and Operations

Streamlining Daily Tasks and Boosting Efficiency with AI

In today's fast-paced business world, efficiency isn't just a nice-to-have—it's a necessity. AI is transforming how businesses operate by streamlining tasks, optimizing workflows, and freeing up valuable time for strategic growth. Whether it's automating routine activities, enhancing productivity with cutting-edge tools, or managing time more effectively, AI has become an indispensable partner in daily operations.

This chapter dives into practical, actionable ways to harness AI for productivity and operational efficiency. You'll learn how to identify and automate repetitive tasks, integrate AI-powered tools into your workflows, and use data-driven insights to make smarter decisions. From improving team collaboration to scaling operations with ease, we'll explore how AI can help you run your business like a well-oiled machine.

By the end of this chapter, you'll have the tools and knowledge to supercharge your operations, reduce stress, and focus on what matters most: growing your business and achieving your goals.

7.1 Automating Routine Tasks with AI

Every business has repetitive tasks that drain time and energy, like data entry, invoice processing, or responding to common customer inquiries. These tasks are essential but often leave you feeling like a hamster on a wheel—running hard without making meaningful progress. The good news? These are the perfect candidates for automation.

To identify tasks that can be automated, take stock of your daily operations. Look for activities that follow a predictable pattern, involve minimal decision-making, or are time-consuming but low in complexity. These might include:

- Data entry and record-keeping

- Managing invoices and payments
- Generating routine reports
- Customer support for frequently asked questions

Once you've pinpointed these tasks, it's time to introduce AI-powered solutions that handle them effortlessly.

Your Business's Best Friend: AI

AI is like a loyal dog—tireless, reliable, and ready to fetch results. Train it well, and it'll save you countless hours while keeping your business running smoothly.

Tools for Task Automation

Enter Robotic Process Automation (RPA) tools and AI-driven virtual assistants—your tireless, error-free digital workforce. These tools streamline repetitive tasks, giving you back valuable time to focus on strategic priorities.

RPA tools act like digital assembly lines, automating actions such as copying data between systems, processing invoices, or managing workflows. Examples include **UiPath** and **Blue Prism**, which provide user-friendly interfaces for automating routine processes without needing advanced coding skills.

AI-driven virtual assistants, such as **Zapier AI** or **Tidio**, excel at customer interaction and task management. They handle scheduling, email responses, and even chatbot interactions, ensuring that routine communication flows smoothly. By integrating these tools into your operations, you'll reduce bottlenecks and eliminate human error from repetitive processes.

Benefits of Automation in Daily Operations

The benefits of automation extend far beyond saving time. Here's how it transforms your operations:

1. **Error Reduction**: Unlike humans, automated systems don't get tired or distracted. They execute tasks with consistent precision, minimizing costly mistakes.

2. **Increased Speed**: Automation accelerates workflows, enabling you to process high volumes of tasks in a fraction of the time.

3. **Scalability**: Automated processes can easily scale with your business, handling more work as you grow without requiring additional staff.

4. **Cost Savings**: By reducing manual labor and inefficiencies, automation cuts costs and boosts your bottom line.

Imagine being able to focus on strategic decisions while AI takes care of the repetitive work, keeping your operations humming along seamlessly.

Integrating Automation into Daily Workflows

Integrating automation into your workflows is easier than you might think. Here's a simple roadmap to get started:

1. **Assess Your Current Processes**: Map out the tasks you want to automate and identify the tools that best fit your needs.

2. **Start Small**: Begin with a single task or workflow to test the waters. Use this as a pilot project to understand the technology and refine the process.

3. **Iterate and Expand**: Gather feedback from your team, adjust as needed, and gradually roll out automation to other areas of your business.

4. **Monitor and Optimize**: Continuously track performance metrics to ensure the automation delivers the desired results. Look for opportunities to further refine and expand your automated processes.

By following this roadmap, you'll integrate automation seamlessly into your daily workflows, boosting productivity and freeing your team to focus on more meaningful work.

Automation Checklist

To guide your automation journey, create a checklist tailored to your business needs:

- *Identify repetitive, time-consuming tasks.*
- *Research automation tools that align with your goals.*
- *Pilot test one process before scaling up.*
- *Train your team using automation tools.*
- *Monitor performance and make iterative improvements.*

This checklist ensures you stay organized and maximizes the benefits of automation while avoiding common pitfalls.

7.2 Enhancing Productivity with AI-Powered Tools

Imagine your business running as smoothly as a symphony, with every team member playing their part in perfect harmony. AI-powered project management tools make this vision a reality by organizing tasks, tracking progress, and ensuring nothing slips through the cracks.

These tools, such as **Asana**, **Monday.com**, or **Trello with AI-enhanced features**, act like digital conductors, helping your team prioritize tasks, set realistic deadlines, and visualize workflows. AI capabilities can even suggest task assignments based on workload and skillsets, ensuring an even distribution of responsibilities. By integrating these tools into your operations, you eliminate the chaos of scattered to-do lists and foster a collaborative environment where everyone knows their role.

Intelligent Scheduling Systems

AI-powered scheduling systems are like having a personal assistant dedicated to optimizing your time. They analyze your calendar, find the best meeting times, and even handle rescheduling conflicts with ease. For instance, tools like **Clockwise** or **Motion** can automatically adjust your schedule to prioritize important tasks while reducing time wastage.

These systems reduce the endless back-and-forth of coordinating meetings and allow you to reclaim hours otherwise spent on logistical headaches. With intelligent scheduling, your day flows effortlessly, enabling you to focus on what truly matters.

Data-Driven Decision-Making with Predictive Analytics

Making informed decisions is often a challenge, but AI turns the tide with predictive analytics. These tools process historical data, analyze patterns, and provide actionable insights to guide your next steps. Platforms like **Looker** and **Power BI** use AI to forecast trends, helping you anticipate challenges and seize opportunities.

Imagine knowing when sales are likely to peak, what customers might want next, or which marketing strategies will yield the best ROI. With predictive analytics, you're no longer guessing—you're acting with confidence, armed with data-driven clarity. AI-based risk assessment tools further enhance decision-making, flagging potential pitfalls before they escalate into problems.

Facilitating Seamless Collaboration

In today's interconnected world, collaboration often involves teams spread across different time zones and working remotely. AI-powered tools ensure that distance is no barrier to productivity. Platforms like **Google Workspace** and **Notion** offer real-time collaboration features enhanced by AI, such as smart document editing and automated version control. You'll never again waste time hunting for the latest version of a file or duplicating efforts.

For meetings, AI-driven tools like **Otter.ai** provide automatic transcription and summaries, ensuring that key points are captured and shared. These capabilities not only improve communication but also foster an environment where everyone stays aligned and informed, regardless of location.

Real-World Examples of AI-Enhanced Productivity

AI-powered tools are already transforming industries. In construction, project management platforms enhanced with AI have improved efficiency by identifying potential bottlenecks and optimizing resource allocation. In retail, scheduling systems powered by AI ensure that staff shifts align with peak customer traffic, reducing costs while maintaining high service levels.

These tools aren't just for large corporations. Small businesses benefit too, with AI making advanced productivity solutions accessible and scalable. Whether you're managing a team of five or fifty, AI ensures you're always running at peak efficiency.

7.3 ChatGPT for Efficient Customer Service

Providing around-the-clock customer service has long been a challenge for businesses. Enter ChatGPT, your digital customer service representative that never sleeps, never takes breaks, and always maintains a friendly tone. Whether it's 3 a.m. or 3 p.m., ChatGPT is available to answer questions, resolve issues, and provide information.

Imagine offering 24/7 support without hiring a night-shift team or outsourcing to a call center. ChatGPT ensures that your customers always have a responsive and helpful resource at their fingertips. It's like having a customer service team that's always energized and never overwhelmed, creating a seamless experience for your audience.

Setting Up ChatGPT for Your Business

Integrating ChatGPT into your business operations is simpler than you might think. Here's how you can get started:

1. **Define Key Use Cases**: Identify the most common customer inquiries or issues, such as order tracking, product information, or refund policies. These will form the foundation of ChatGPT's interactions.

2. **Create Response Templates**: Develop standardized, brand-aligned templates for common questions. For example:

    - **Order Status Inquiry**: "Sure, let me check that for you. Could you provide your order number?"

    - **Returns Policy**: "Our return policy allows you to send back items within 30 days. Would you like help initiating a return?" Templates ensure consistent responses across interactions.

3. **Train ChatGPT on Your Business**: Input details about your products, services, and policies so ChatGPT can provide accurate and specific responses. Think of it as teaching an employee all they need to know about your business.

4. **Integrate with Existing Systems**: Connect ChatGPT to your website, e-commerce platform, or CRM software to streamline interactions. Tools like **Zapier** make integrations straightforward, allowing ChatGPT to access order histories or customer data.

Benefits of AI-Driven Customer Service

Deploying ChatGPT as part of your customer service strategy offers numerous advantages:

- **Immediate Responses**: ChatGPT handles inquiries instantly, eliminating long wait times and keeping customers engaged.
- **Cost Efficiency**: Automating routine interactions reduces the need for additional staff, freeing your team to focus on complex or high-value tasks.
- **Scalability**: Whether you have 10 or 10,000 customers, ChatGPT scales effortlessly to meet demand without compromising quality.
- **Consistent Quality**: Unlike human agents who may vary in tone or knowledge, ChatGPT provides uniform, brand-aligned responses every time.

Real-World Applications of ChatGPT in Customer Service

Businesses across industries are leveraging ChatGPT to enhance their customer service:

- **E-Commerce**: Online retailers use ChatGPT to handle inquiries during busy shopping seasons. From answering product questions to resolving cart issues, ChatGPT ensures a smooth customer journey.
- **Hospitality**: Hotels and travel agencies employ ChatGPT to automate booking processes and respond to guest inquiries, streamlining operations and improving guest satisfaction.
- **Healthcare**: Clinics use ChatGPT to manage appointment scheduling, reducing administrative workloads and improving patient access to care.

Extending ChatGPT's Capabilities

Beyond answering questions, ChatGPT can be programmed for more advanced functionalities, such as:

- **Proactive Customer Engagement**: ChatGPT can initiate conversations, offering assistance before customers need to ask.

For example, a pop-up chat might appear on an e-commerce site saying, "Looking for help with your order?"

- **Language Translation**: Multilingual capabilities allow businesses to serve diverse audiences, breaking down language barriers and expanding customer reach.
- **Sales Assistance**: ChatGPT can suggest products based on customer preferences, acting as a virtual salesperson that never misses an upsell opportunity.

Scalability and Versatility

The versatility of ChatGPT ensures that it adapts to your business needs as they grow. While it handles routine queries, your human team can focus on resolving more complex issues. This hybrid approach enhances overall efficiency, delivering a superior customer experience.

7.4 Streamlining Business Operations with AI

Managing a supply chain can often feel like navigating a maze, with countless variables influencing timing, costs, and efficiency. AI steps in as your trusted guide, analyzing data across the supply chain to predict demand, optimize routes, and ensure smooth operations. It's like having a logistics expert on your team who never sleeps.

AI-powered tools can identify potential disruptions—whether it's a delayed shipment or a supplier issue—before they escalate, enabling proactive adjustments. For example, predictive algorithms can flag likely delays due to weather or inventory shortages, helping you reroute shipments or adjust production schedules to maintain a steady flow of goods.

Inventory Management

Keeping inventory levels balanced is critical to avoiding stockouts or overstock situations. AI helps by analyzing sales trends, customer behavior, and seasonal fluctuations to predict demand with precision. Think of it as a crystal ball for your inventory.

AI can automate stock replenishment by integrating directly with your point-of-sale system. For example:

- **Low Stock Alerts**: AI can notify you when inventory reaches a critical threshold.

- **Automated Reorders**: It can place orders automatically for high-demand items, ensuring shelves are always stocked with what customers want.

This reduces waste, minimizes carrying costs, and ensures your customers find what they need when they need it.

Quality Control

Quality control is an area where AI truly shines. Unlike humans who may miss subtle defects, AI systems use advanced image recognition and sensor technology to identify inconsistencies in products with pinpoint accuracy. For example:

- **Automated Inspections**: AI-powered cameras can scan products on a production line, identifying defects in real-time.
- **Predictive Maintenance**: AI can monitor equipment performance and predict potential failures before they occur, ensuring minimal downtime and consistent product quality.

By improving quality assurance processes, businesses can reduce costly recalls, enhance customer satisfaction, and build a reputation for reliability.

AI-Powered Logistics and Workflow Management

AI transforms logistics from a complex puzzle into a seamless operation. By optimizing delivery routes and schedules, AI reduces transit times and cuts fuel costs, making your operations both efficient and eco-friendly. For example:

- **Dynamic Routing**: AI systems adjust delivery routes in real-time based on traffic, weather, or other factors to ensure timely arrivals.
- **Fleet Management**: AI helps allocate vehicles and drivers effectively, ensuring resources are used optimally.

Workflow management tools powered by AI streamline operations within your business. These systems coordinate tasks, manage schedules, and improve communication across departments. It's like having a digital conductor orchestrating every part of your business to perform in harmony.

Reducing Operational Costs with AI

AI-driven efficiency leads directly to cost savings. By identifying areas of waste—such as excess energy use or redundant processes—AI helps businesses save money and reduce their environmental impact. For example:

- **Energy Optimization**: AI monitors energy usage across facilities, suggesting adjustments that lower consumption without impacting performance.
- **Material Waste Reduction**: By analyzing production data, AI identifies inefficiencies and recommends ways to minimize scrap or surplus.

These savings free up resources that can be reinvested into growth opportunities, making AI a powerful ally for sustainable and cost-effective operations.

Real-World Examples of AI-Enhanced Operations

AI is transforming industries worldwide with tangible results:

- **Manufacturing**: Factories use AI to monitor machinery, automate workflows, and ensure production lines run smoothly. For example, predictive maintenance reduces equipment downtime, while AI-powered quality checks enhance output consistency.
- **Retail**: Retailers rely on AI to optimize inventory, ensuring popular products are always in stock and reducing waste on items with slower turnover. Automated restocking systems allow businesses to focus on customer service rather than logistics.

The Role of AI as an Operational Efficiency Hero

AI is more than a tool—it's a partner in efficiency. From optimizing supply chains to improving quality control, AI enables businesses to operate at peak performance with minimal waste. By embracing AI-driven solutions, you can focus on strategic growth while leaving routine operational challenges in the capable hands of technology.

Streamlining Operations with AI

***Objective**: Help readers systematically identify and implement AI solutions for productivity and operations.*

***Steps**:*

1. *Identify areas of inefficiency in your business.*

2. *Match inefficiencies with AI tools (e.g., RPA for repetitive tasks, predictive analytics for inventory).*

3. *Pilot-test AI solutions on a small scale.*

4. *Integrate AI tools into daily workflows and monitor performance.*

5. *Iterate and optimize based on feedback.*

7.5 Managing Time Effectively Using AI Solutions

Time is one of the most valuable resources in any business, and AI is here to help you make the most of it. Intelligent calendar apps act as your personal assistant, effortlessly organizing meetings, deadlines, and reminders. These apps analyze your schedule, finding optimal slots for appointments and flagging potential conflicts before they arise. For example:

- **Smart Scheduling**: Tools like Calendly integrate with your calendar to suggest meeting times based on availability.

- **Task Prioritization**: AI-driven to-do lists, such as Todoist with AI features, rank tasks by urgency and importance, ensuring you tackle the most critical items first.

These tools help you transition from reactive time management—constantly putting out fires—to a proactive approach where you're always one step ahead.

Reducing Time Wastage with AI

AI tools help identify and eliminate hidden time wasters in your workflow. Automated time trackers analyze how you spend your day, pinpointing unproductive habits like excessive email checking or meeting overload. For example:

- **Time Tracking Insights**: Platforms like RescueTime provide detailed reports on your daily activities, showing where your time goes and how to reclaim it.
- **Focus Assistants**: Tools like Focus@Will use AI to curate music or soundscapes that enhance concentration, helping you dive into deep work and stay there.

By gaining a clear picture of your time usage, you can make informed adjustments, streamlining your day and boosting productivity.

Integrating AI into Time Management Routines

Incorporating AI into your daily routine doesn't require a major overhaul. Small changes, like enabling AI-driven reminders or syncing your task manager with your email, can make a big impact. Here's how to get started:

1. **Set Automated Reminders**: Use tools like Microsoft Outlook or Google Calendar to schedule recurring tasks or nudge you about deadlines.
2. **Customize Notifications**: Tailor alerts to focus only on high-priority events or tasks, reducing interruptions.
3. **Combine Tools**: Sync AI-powered task prioritization tools with your calendar for seamless integration.

These small tweaks enhance existing habits, making your workflow more efficient without overwhelming you with new systems to learn.

Achieving Work-Life Balance with AI

One of the most overlooked benefits of AI in time management is its role in maintaining a healthy work-life balance. AI can help by:

- **Scheduling Downtime**: Tools like Clockwise automatically block out "focus time" or personal time, ensuring your calendar isn't overrun with back-to-back meetings.

- **Reducing Stress**: By automating repetitive tasks and organizing your day, AI reduces the cognitive load, allowing you to focus on higher-value activities.

A balanced approach to time management doesn't just improve your productivity—it enhances your overall well-being, making you a more effective and satisfied business owner.

Wrapping Up Time Management with AI

AI-driven time management tools transform how you organize your day, enabling precision and reducing stress. From smart scheduling to focus-enhancing solutions, these tools free you to concentrate on high-value tasks while ensuring your personal time remains protected. By incorporating AI into your routine, you can achieve a healthier balance and greater productivity.

7.6 Summary

AI is revolutionizing the way businesses operate, making productivity and efficiency accessible to companies of all sizes. From automating routine tasks to optimizing supply chains and managing time effectively, AI equips you with tools to streamline daily operations and focus on strategic growth. The result is a business that runs like a finely tuned machine, leaving you free to innovate and thrive.

With these tools, you can transform your operations, reclaim your time, and focus on innovation. Start small, automate one task today, and watch the results snowball.

But the power of AI doesn't stop at internal operations. In the next chapter, we'll explore how AI can supercharge your marketing strategies, helping you reach the right audience, craft personalized messages, and convert leads into loyal customers. Get ready to harness AI's potential to take your marketing efforts to the next level!

A Word from the Author

I hope this journey into unlocking AI's potential for your business has sparked ideas, solutions, and maybe even a bit of excitement about the possibilities ahead. If you're finding the content useful or inspiring, I would greatly appreciate hearing your thoughts.

Your feedback helps other entrepreneurs discover this resource and start their own journey to smarter, AI-driven success. A quick review on Amazon can make a real difference—helping others transform their businesses while supporting the creation of future tools and insights.

Thank you for taking a moment to share your experience and for being part of the AI-powered revolution for small businesses!

Scan this QR Code…

Amazon Review
Unlocking Artificial Intelligence for Entrepreneur Success
https://www.amazon.com/review/create-review/?asin=1964520088

Chapter 8: Innovative AI-Driven Marketing

Creating Deeper Connections and Smarter Strategies

Step into a world where marketing doesn't just reach customers—it resonates with them. Every message feels tailored, every interaction seamless, and every product perfectly aligned with a customer's needs. This isn't a distant dream; it's the reality AI is creating for businesses today. With the power of AI, marketing is no longer about broadcasting to the masses—it's about building connections that feel personal and meaningful.

In this chapter, we'll explore how AI is transforming marketing from a general strategy to a precision-based art form. From identifying distinct customer segments to delivering personalized content and dynamically adjusting pricing, AI enables smarter, more efficient campaigns. You'll learn how AI tools analyze vast amounts of data to uncover actionable insights, predict trends, and adapt strategies in real time. And with tools like ChatGPT, creating engaging, consistent content across platforms becomes effortless.

Marketing is evolving, and AI is the catalyst driving this change. Whether you're looking to make a big splash or refine your existing strategies, this chapter will show you how to harness AI's potential to create memorable, results-driven marketing experiences.

8.1 Audience Segmentation

Imagine having a personal assistant who not only knows your customers but also understands their individual needs, habits, and preferences. That's what AI brings to audience segmentation—the ability to analyze mountains of data and uncover patterns that transform broad customer groups into precise, meaningful segments. It's like having a digital tailor who creates perfectly fitted marketing strategies for each customer, based not just on age or income but on behaviors, preferences, and even geographic location.

Behavioral and Geographic Targeting

Let's say you run an online bookstore. With AI, you can analyze your customers' purchase histories to identify who prefers thrillers and who loves cozy mysteries. This behavioral targeting lets you send personalized recommendations, like suggesting the latest crime novel to your thriller enthusiasts. It's like handing them a treasure map to their next favorite read.

Geographic targeting takes this a step further by using location data to craft messages that resonate with specific audiences. For instance, a bakery might promote its seasonal pumpkin spice muffins to customers in cooler climates while highlighting refreshing iced treats to those in warmer regions. This isn't about tracking your customers' every move—it's about understanding their context and delivering value at just the right moment. AI transforms marketing from a guessing game into an experience that feels custom-made, helping you connect with your audience on a deeper level.

8.2 Personalization of Content Delivery

Personalization of content delivery is where AI truly shines, turning dry marketing messages into engaging conversations. AI enables dynamic content adaptation, ensuring each email or message feels custom-made for the recipient.

Product Recommendations

Personalized product recommendations act like a shopping assistant that knows your style, enhancing the shopping experience and driving sales by analyzing browsing behavior and purchase history.

8.3 AI-Driven Dynamic Pricing Models

Let's explore AI-driven dynamic pricing models—the secret sauce for maximizing revenue while keeping customers happy. Picture a world where prices adjust in real-time, responding to shifts in consumer demand and behavior. During a flash sale, AI ensures prices remain competitive yet profitable, much like a savvy negotiator who knows exactly when to strike the perfect deal.

Loyalty-based pricing schemes take customer relationships into account by offering discounts to frequent buyers, fostering a sense of appreciation and loyalty. It's like a secret handshake for your best customers, rewarding them for their continued support and encouraging them to come back again and again.

To illustrate the power of AI personalization, let's look at some real-world success stories:

- **Streaming Services** have mastered the art of customizing content suggestions. By analyzing individual viewing habits, they recommend shows and movies that align with personal preferences, transforming endless scrolling into a tailored entertainment experience. This isn't just about engagement; it's about building loyalty and reducing churn.

- **Retailers** have embraced AI to create personalized shopping experiences. Through analyzing customer data, they develop marketing messages that resonate on a personal level, turning browsers into buyers. Imagine having a personal shopper who knows exactly what you want, making every visit feel special and satisfying.

Interactive Element: Personalization Audit

Take a moment to list three areas in your marketing strategy where personalization could make a difference. Consider how AI could enhance these areas—whether it's through targeted messaging, dynamic pricing, or personalized recommendations. Reflect on the tools you might need and the data you could leverage to bring these ideas to life.

AI in marketing is not just a trend; it's a revolution that's reshaping how businesses engage with their audiences. By leveraging AI for audience segmentation, personalized content delivery, and dynamic pricing, you can create marketing experiences that are as unique as your customers. This isn't just about selling; it's about building relationships that last, ensuring your business thrives in a competitive landscape.

AI-Driven Marketing in Action

Objective*: Use AI tools to craft and execute personalized, data-driven marketing strategies that connect with your audience and drive results.*

Steps:

1. ***Define Your Marketing Goals**: Start with a clear objective. Are you trying to increase engagement, drive conversions, or improve customer retention? Be specific about what success looks like.*
   ***Example**: "Help me brainstorm strategies to improve email open rates for my e-commerce store."*

2. ***Segment Your Audience**: Use AI tools like HubSpot or Customer.io to group your audience based on demographics, behaviors, or preferences.*
   ***Example**: "What are effective ways to segment customers for a fitness apparel brand?"*

3. ***Generate Personalized Content**: Leverage AI tools like ChatGPT, Copy.ai, or Jasper to create tailored messages for each segment.*
   ***Example**: "Write a friendly and engaging email for customers who've purchased running shoes, offering tips for improving their pace."*

4. ***Explore Dynamic Pricing Models**: Test dynamic pricing with tools like Revionics or Prisync to match price points with demand, seasonality, or competitor trends.*
   ***Example**: "Suggest a dynamic pricing strategy for an online bookstore during holiday sales."*

5. ***Analyze Data and Refine Strategies**: Use predictive analytics and feedback to measure success. Tools like Google Analytics and Sprout Social can provide actionable insights.*
   ***Example**: "Analyze customer feedback to identify areas for improving a subscription meal delivery service."*

6. ***Test and Optimize**: A/B test variations of your campaigns using AI tools to see what resonates best with your audience.*
   ***Example**: "Design two variations of a Facebook ad for a coffee subscription box to test engagement rates."*

Tips for Success

- **Start Small**: Focus on one or two campaigns to avoid overwhelm and build confidence.
- **Iterate Often**: Use feedback to refine your strategies and maximize impact.
- **Track Metrics**: Keep an eye on KPIs (key performance indicators) to measure the effectiveness of your AI-driven marketing.

8.4 Data-Driven Insights for Smarter Marketing

Imagine stepping into the shoes of a detective, piecing together clues to understand your customers and the ever-changing market landscape. AI tools act as your magnifying glass, offering a sharper and more comprehensive view of consumer behavior, trends, and preferences. Like Sherlock Holmes solving a mystery, AI helps you uncover insights that were once hidden in plain sight.

The Crystal Ball of Marketing

Think of AI as your marketing oracle—armed with data, it predicts trends and reveals customer desires before they're even spoken. It's not magic, but it's close!

Gathering Data: Web Analytics and Social Media Listening

Every interaction a customer has with your brand leaves behind a trail of data. AI-enabled tools are designed to follow these trails and make sense of the patterns they reveal.

Web Analytics Platforms

Think of tools like Google Analytics as your trusty sidekicks, tirelessly tracking every click, scroll, and linger on your website. They offer a backstage pass to your customers' journeys, showing you what captivates their attention and where they lose interest. For example, if most visitors abandon their carts on the checkout page, web analytics can spotlight the problem, whether it's high shipping costs or a clunky user experience. Armed with these insights, you can refine your website to boost conversions and keep customers engaged.

Social Media Listening

Now, imagine eavesdropping on the world's largest conversation about your brand. Tools like Hootsuite and Brandwatch do just that by scanning social media posts, reviews, and comments to gauge public sentiment. It's like having a spy who reports back on customer perceptions—what they love, what frustrates them, and what they're talking about in real-time. This treasure trove of insights allows you to respond to concerns, celebrate positive feedback, and keep your finger on the pulse of your audience.

Analyzing Data: Predictive Analytics and Sentiment Analysis

Once data is gathered, AI steps in to help you decode the story it's telling.

Predictive Analytics

AI uses predictive analytics to transform raw data into foresight. Much like a skilled fortune teller reading tea leaves, predictive models examine past customer behaviors to forecast future trends. For instance, an online retailer might notice that sales for winter jackets consistently spike in late October. With predictive analytics, they can plan inventory and launch promotions ahead of time, ensuring they meet demand seamlessly.

Sentiment Analysis

If predictive analytics is the fortune teller, sentiment analysis is your emotional barometer. It sifts through reviews, tweets, and other brand mentions to determine how customers feel about your products or services. Whether customers are raving about a new feature or voicing frustration over delays, sentiment analysis helps you adapt your messaging and customer service to maintain a positive brand image.

Forecasting: Demand and Trend Predictions

AI takes forecasting to the next level by helping you stay ahead of the curve.

Demand Forecasting

Using historical sales data, AI models can predict when specific products will experience increased demand. For example, a grocery chain might learn that sales of iced coffee surge during heatwaves, allowing them to stock up and advertise accordingly. By anticipating customer needs, you can ensure that your inventory aligns with demand, reducing both overstock and missed opportunities.

Trend Prediction

In industries like fashion or wellness, staying ahead of emerging trends is key to maintaining relevance. AI identifies subtle shifts in consumer behavior, like growing interest in sustainable materials or plant-based diets, long before they become mainstream. By positioning your business as a leader rather than a follower, you can capture attention and loyalty in a competitive market.

Real-World Success Stories

Automotive Industry

Car manufacturers are using AI to analyze consumer preferences, from safety features to eco-friendly options. These insights help them design and market vehicles that align with shifting customer demands, ensuring their offerings remain compelling.

Food Industry

Food brands are leveraging AI to adjust their marketing strategies in line with emerging dietary trends, such as the growing popularity of plant-based and gluten-free products. This not only keeps them relevant but also fosters trust and connection with health-conscious consumers.

Data-Driven Strategy Planner

To put these insights into practice, reflect on the data you already collect in your business.

- *What do your current analytics tools tell you about your customers?*
- *Which areas of your marketing strategy could benefit from a deeper understanding or more accurate forecasting?*
- *Consider how AI tools like predictive analytics or sentiment analysis could transform your approach.*

Use this exercise as a roadmap to integrate AI into your data analysis and strategy development, ensuring your marketing decisions are always informed, proactive, and impactful.

8.5 Crafting Engaging Content with ChatGPT

Picture this: you're sipping your morning coffee, pondering how to keep your content fresh and your audience engaged. Enter ChatGPT, your digital brainstorm buddy, ready to whip up engaging material while you finish that muffin. Whether you're staring at a blank screen, hoping for inspiration, or juggling multiple platforms, ChatGPT becomes your creative partner, generating ideas and delivering polished drafts without ever running out of energy or patience.

Blog Post Generation

Let's start with blog posts, the backbone of many content strategies. ChatGPT can transform a rough idea into a polished draft in record time. Imagine you're tasked with writing about a niche topic like sustainable fashion or emerging tech trends. Instead of wrestling with writer's block, you input a few key points, and ChatGPT does the heavy lifting. It breaks down complex topics into clear, readable content, ensuring your brand's tone and style remain consistent. Think of it as having a ghostwriter who works at the speed of light, enabling you to produce high-quality blogs that keep your audience coming back for more.

Social Media Campaign Copywriting

Social media campaigns require short, punchy content that grabs attention and drives engagement. ChatGPT excels here, crafting posts tailored to different platforms and audiences. It's like having a social media manager who's always up-to-date on trends and algorithms. Whether you need a witty tweet, a captivating Instagram caption, or a professional LinkedIn post, ChatGPT delivers content that resonates. By automating this aspect of content creation, you can maintain an active and engaging social presence without spending countless hours brainstorming and editing.

Ensuring Brand Consistency Across Platforms

Your brand's voice is its signature, and consistency across platforms is key to building trust and loyalty. ChatGPT ensures every piece of content aligns with your brand's tone, whether it's formal, playful, or somewhere in between. Imagine a customer reading your blog, then receiving a promotional email, and finally seeing a social media post—all carrying the same voice and message. This seamless experience reinforces your brand identity, making your business feel reliable and cohesive, like a trusted friend who's always on point.

Boosting Content Production Efficiency

The content demands of modern marketing can feel overwhelming. Maintaining a robust content calendar without burning out is no small feat, especially for small teams. ChatGPT lightens the load by streamlining production workflows. Need a week's worth of social media posts, a blog draft, and an email newsletter? ChatGPT can help you produce it all in a fraction of the time. By automating repetitive or labor-intensive tasks, you free up energy for strategic thinking and creative pursuits, all while keeping your audience engaged with fresh content.

Real-Time Content Adaptation

One of ChatGPT's standout features is its ability to adapt content in real time. Imagine covering a live event, like a product launch or industry conference. As the event unfolds, you need to update your audience quickly and accurately. ChatGPT can process real-time data and generate updates that keep your followers informed and engaged. It's like having a newsroom on standby, ready to deliver breaking news with precision and speed.

Global and Culturally Adaptive Content

Reaching a global audience requires sensitivity to cultural nuances and preferences. ChatGPT shines here, crafting content that resonates with diverse readers. For example, a marketing campaign for an international audience might require adjustments to language, tone, and even imagery to appeal to local tastes. ChatGPT helps tailor your messaging for each region, ensuring it's both relevant and respectful. Whether you're connecting with customers in Tokyo, Toronto, or Timbuktu, ChatGPT bridges cultural gaps, making your brand feel accessible and inclusive.

8.6 Summary

In this chapter, we've journeyed through the ways AI is revolutionizing marketing. By segmenting audiences, delivering hyper-personalized content, and optimizing pricing strategies, you can create campaigns that resonate deeply with your customers. AI tools enable you to analyze data, predict trends, and adapt strategies in real time, ensuring your marketing efforts are always on point. Whether you're leveraging AI to craft engaging content or using it to predict customer behavior, the opportunities to enhance your marketing have never been more accessible or exciting.

But creating innovative marketing campaigns is just the beginning. The real challenge—and opportunity—lies in turning that engagement into lasting relationships. How do you keep customers coming back, proactively meet their needs, and foster loyalty in a crowded marketplace?

In the next chapter, we'll explore how AI empowers you to move beyond marketing and build meaningful connections. From analyzing feedback to creating personalized interactions, you'll learn how to use AI to deepen customer relationships and ensure your business stays top-of-mind. Get ready to turn interest into lasting loyalty, one AI-driven interaction at a time.

Chapter 9: Maximizing Customer Engagement

Enhancing Customer Experiences with Personalized and Predictive Strategies

In today's competitive business landscape, customer relationships are more than just transactions—they are the foundation of long-term success. The ability to understand, anticipate, and respond to customer needs can set a business apart, and AI is making this more achievable than ever before. From analyzing feedback to delivering personalized experiences, AI empowers businesses to forge deeper connections with their customers.

This chapter explores how AI can transform your approach to customer engagement. You'll discover practical ways to leverage AI tools for analyzing feedback, personalizing interactions, and creating proactive engagement strategies. Whether you're running a small shop or managing a growing enterprise, these techniques can help you build loyalty, strengthen relationships, and enhance your customers' overall experience. Let's dive into the possibilities AI offers to make every customer interaction meaningful and impactful.

9.1: Understanding Customer Feedback with AI

Customer feedback is one of the most valuable resources a business can tap into. Every review, comment, or survey response provides a glimpse into your customers' thoughts, revealing what they value most and where they see room for improvement. But manually sifting through mountains of feedback can be overwhelming. This is where AI steps in, transforming raw feedback into actionable insights.

Uncovering Emotions with Sentiment Analysis

AI-driven sentiment analysis allows you to measure positive, neutral, or negative customer emotions across large volumes of feedback. By identifying trends and common themes, you can better understand how your customers feel about your products or services and why they feel that way.

For example, consider a local coffee shop receiving dozens of reviews monthly. Instead of combing through each comment manually, an AI tool can quickly summarize the sentiment behind the reviews. It might highlight consistent praise for the smoothness of your lattes while pointing out recurring complaints about wait times. These insights give you a clear roadmap for refining your offerings and addressing pain points, ensuring you consistently meet and exceed customer expectations.

Accessible Tools for Every Business

You don't need to be a tech wizard to leverage AI for sentiment analysis. Platforms like **MonkeyLearn** and **Repustate** offer no-code solutions that are affordable, user-friendly, and tailored to small business needs. These tools allow you to quickly process customer feedback and extract valuable insights without technical expertise.

Turning Insights into Action

Understanding what your customers love and where they encounter challenges is the first step toward building stronger relationships. By acting on the insights provided by AI-driven sentiment analysis, you can create a more responsive and customer-focused business. Whether you're addressing a common complaint or doubling down on what your customers already adore, AI ensures that every decision is informed by real, actionable feedback.

This is not just about gathering data; it's about using that data to create a better customer experience, one insight at a time.

9.2: Personalizing Customer Interactions

In today's competitive market, personalization is no longer a luxury—it's an expectation. Customers want experiences that feel tailored specifically to them, and AI offers the tools to make this a reality. By leveraging AI, businesses can craft interactions that are not only relevant but also meaningful, fostering stronger connections and higher customer satisfaction.

AI in Personalized Marketing

AI enables businesses to segment audiences based on behavior, preferences, and purchase history, creating opportunities for more targeted and impactful marketing. Instead of sending generic messages, you can deliver content that speaks directly to a customer's unique interests.

For instance, a small bookstore can use AI to analyze a reader's past purchases and recommend books in a similar genre. If a customer enjoyed a gripping thriller, the system might suggest other thrillers by related authors or in a comparable style. These personalized recommendations make the interaction feel thoughtful and curated, turning casual shoppers into loyal patrons.

Enhancing Interactions with Chatbots and Recommendation Systems

Chatbots powered by AI, such as ChatGPT, take customer support and engagement to the next level. These bots can handle routine questions, recommend products, and even adapt their conversational style to align with customer profiles. The result is an experience that feels seamless and interactive, as if customers are speaking to a knowledgeable and attentive assistant.

Imagine a boutique using a chatbot to assist with product queries. Beyond answering questions like "Do you have this item in stock?" the bot could analyze the customer's browsing behavior and suggest complementary items. For example, if a customer is looking at a dress, the chatbot might recommend matching accessories or shoes. This level of personalization not only enhances the shopping experience but also boosts conversions by guiding customers toward additional purchases.

The Impact of Personalization

By personalizing customer interactions, businesses create experiences that resonate with their audience on a deeper level. AI transforms generic outreach into meaningful connections, ensuring every customer feels seen and valued. Whether it's through tailored recommendations or responsive chatbots, personalization drives engagement, builds loyalty, and ultimately contributes to lasting business success.

Your Customer Relationship Whisperer

Think of AI as your business's whisperer—quietly listening to customer needs, predicting their wants, and helping you deliver beyond their expectations.

9.3: Enhancing Customer Service with AI

Customer service is at the heart of building loyalty and trust, and AI can play a transformative role in enhancing the customer experience. By automating routine tasks, AI ensures quicker responses while freeing your team to focus on complex, high-value interactions. The result is a seamless service experience that satisfies both efficiency and personalization.

Automated Customer Support

AI-powered chatbots have become indispensable tools for 24/7 customer service. They excel at handling routine queries such as "What are your store hours?" or "Where is my order?" These chatbots operate tirelessly, ensuring customers receive immediate responses regardless of the time of day.

Far from replacing human agents, chatbots augment your support team by managing repetitive tasks. This division of labor allows human representatives to dedicate their time and expertise to resolving more nuanced issues, enhancing the overall service quality.

Smart Escalation for Complex Issues

Not all customer concerns can be resolved by AI alone. A well-designed AI system recognizes its limitations and knows when to escalate an issue to a human representative. This escalation process ensures that customers with complex needs or sensitive concerns receive the personal attention they deserve.

For example, consider a small e-commerce shop using a chatbot to address frequently asked questions. When a customer requests a refund or reports a defective product, the chatbot can seamlessly route the case to a human agent, preserving the personal touch for critical moments. This balance between automation and human engagement maintains service quality while improving efficiency.

The Benefits of AI-Enhanced Customer Service

AI in customer service offers businesses the best of both worlds: speed and scalability. Customers benefit from prompt resolutions to routine inquiries, while your team can focus on high-impact issues. By integrating AI into your customer service strategy, you ensure a responsive, efficient, and empathetic experience that leaves a lasting positive impression.

9.4: Proactively Engaging Customers

Customer engagement is most effective when it's not just reactive but anticipatory. AI transforms engagement into a proactive strategy, helping you anticipate customer needs, reconnect with inactive customers, and build loyalty through personalized outreach. By using predictive algorithms and re-engagement campaigns, you can show your customers that you understand their preferences and are actively working to meet their expectations.

Predictive Engagement

AI thrives on data, using patterns in customer behavior to forecast their needs before they even realize them. Predictive engagement tools can analyze purchasing habits, browsing history, and seasonal trends to deliver timely, relevant interactions.

For instance, a skincare brand might leverage AI to send restocking reminders for products that customers typically repurchase. These proactive messages not only provide convenience but also demonstrate attentiveness, fostering a stronger customer connection. Whether it's reminding a customer to reorder a favorite product or suggesting items for an upcoming holiday, predictive engagement positions your brand as one step ahead, enhancing trust and loyalty.

Re-Engagement Campaigns

Sometimes, customers drift away—whether due to competing priorities or simple forgetfulness. AI tools can help you identify these lapsed customers and develop personalized strategies to re-engage them. By analyzing historical data, AI can pinpoint patterns in customer inactivity and craft targeted campaigns that rekindle interest.

For example, a fitness studio could use AI to track members who haven't attended a class in several weeks. A tailored email might remind them of upcoming sessions or offer a discount to encourage their return. This targeted approach not only brings back lost customers but also reinforces your brand's commitment to their satisfaction and well-being.

The Value of Proactive Engagement

Proactively engaging customers isn't just about making the next sale—it's about building relationships. AI enables businesses to go beyond reacting to customer needs, positioning them as trusted partners in their customers' journeys. By anticipating desires and maintaining meaningful connections, your business can foster loyalty and stand out in an increasingly competitive landscape.

9.5: Using Data to Drive Customer Engagement Strategy

AI doesn't just enhance customer engagement—it empowers you with insights to continuously improve your approach. By leveraging AI-driven data analysis, you can refine your strategies, ensuring every interaction aligns with your audience's preferences and needs. From precise customer segmentation to tracking key engagement metrics, AI transforms raw data into actionable strategies.

Customer Segmentation

Effective engagement begins with understanding your audience. AI enables you to segment customers based on diverse factors, such as demographics, purchasing habits, or online behaviors. By categorizing customers into meaningful groups, you can create tailored messages that resonate with each segment's unique preferences.

For example, a bakery might segment its customers into groups like "frequent buyers" and "seasonal shoppers." AI can then help craft targeted promotions for each group—such as loyalty rewards for regular customers or holiday-themed discounts for occasional visitors. This personalized approach not only drives sales but also strengthens customer loyalty, as each segment feels understood and valued.

Engagement Metrics and Tracking

To refine your engagement strategies, it's crucial to measure their effectiveness. AI tools track key engagement metrics, including email open rates, click-through rates, response times, and more. These insights reveal what resonates with your audience and highlight areas for improvement.

Consider a real estate agent using AI to monitor response times to customer inquiries. By analyzing this data, they might identify delays and implement systems to ensure prompt follow-ups. This focus on responsiveness enhances the customer experience, fostering trust and professionalism. Similarly, tracking metrics like email engagement can help fine-tune messaging for greater impact, ensuring future campaigns achieve their goals.

Transforming Insights into Action

The power of AI lies in its ability to turn data into actionable insights. With AI-driven tools, you're not just collecting information—you're uncovering patterns and opportunities to better connect with your audience. By segmenting customers effectively and analyzing engagement metrics, you can refine your approach, ensuring your strategies remain dynamic, impactful, and aligned with your customers' evolving needs.

Your AI Engagement Starter Plan

Starting with AI for customer engagement doesn't have to be overwhelming. Follow this step-by-step guide to integrate AI into your business in a manageable and impactful way. Use this plan as a checklist to ensure a smooth and successful start.

Step 1: Select Beginner-Friendly AI Tools

Choose tools that are easy to use and require little to no technical expertise. For example, platforms like ChatGPT for conversational AI or MonkeyLearn for sentiment analysis are great starting points. These tools are designed for beginners, allowing you to see results without needing extensive training or setup.

Your Task: *Research and list three AI tools that align with your business needs. Look for features like ease of use, compatibility with existing platforms, and customer support availability.*

Step 2: Integrate with Existing Platforms

Maximize efficiency by connecting AI tools to platforms you already use, such as WordPress, HubSpot, or MailChimp. Integration streamlines workflows and lets you quickly see the impact of AI on your operations.

Your Task: *Identify which of your current platforms offer AI integration options. Explore their documentation or support resources to understand the integration process.*

Step 3: Start with Budget-Conscious Options
Many AI tools offer free trials or affordable pricing tiers, making them accessible for small businesses. Begin with these cost-effective solutions to test their impact and scalability.

Your Task*: Compare pricing tiers for your shortlisted tools. Take advantage of free trials or starter plans to evaluate the value AI brings to your business before making a larger investment.*

This structured approach helps you ease into AI implementation, focusing on tools and strategies that fit your business size and needs. By starting small and scaling as you see results, you can confidently integrate AI into your customer engagement processes and reap the benefits of smarter, more efficient strategies.

AI-Powered Customer Engagement

Objective*: Use AI tools to build stronger, more personalized relationships with your customers, driving engagement and loyalty.*

Steps:

1. ***Collect Customer Feedback****: Use AI-powered sentiment analysis tools like MonkeyLearn or Qualtrics to gather insights from surveys, reviews, and social media.*
   Example*: "Analyze customer reviews for a coffee shop and identify the top three recurring themes."*

2. ***Segment Your Customers****: Group customers based on behaviors, preferences, and past interactions using AI tools like HubSpot or Salesforce.*
   Example*: "Segment customers of an online bookstore into groups based on purchase history and browsing habits."*

3. ***Create Personalized Campaigns****: Use ChatGPT or Jasper to craft tailored messages for each customer segment.*
   Example*: "Write a friendly email to loyal customers of a bakery offering a sneak peek of new menu items."*

4. ***Enhance Customer Service with AI***: *Implement AI chatbots like Tidio or Intercom to handle common queries and escalate complex issues to human agents.*
   Example: *"Act as a customer service chatbot for a clothing store, handling a question about return policies."*

5. ***Proactively Re-Engage Customers***: *Use predictive analytics to identify at-risk customers and design campaigns to re-engage them.*
   Example: *"Generate a re-engagement email for customers who haven't purchased in six months."*

6. ***Track Metrics and Refine Strategies***: *Monitor engagement metrics (e.g., click-through rates, customer satisfaction scores) using AI tools like Google Analytics or Zoho CRM. Use this data to refine your strategies.*
   Example: *"What are the key engagement metrics for a subscription box service, and how can we improve them?"*

Tips for Success

- **Start Small**: Focus on one touchpoint, such as email marketing or customer service, and expand as you see results.

- **Iterate Continuously**: Use customer feedback and data insights to refine your approach.

- **Be Human-Centric**: Even with AI, prioritize empathy and understanding in all customer interactions.

9.6 AI Engagement Starter Plan

With the insights from this chapter, you're ready to take action. The following Starter Plan Playbook provides a step-by-step framework to help you apply AI to enhance customer engagement effectively.

Making the Most of the Plan

- Start small: Choose one area of engagement to focus on, such as email campaigns or customer service.

- Iterate and improve: Use feedback and data to refine your approach over time.

- Stay customer-centric: Remember, AI is here to enhance the human touch, not replace it.

This starter plan is your roadmap to stronger customer relationships. The tools and strategies are within your reach—now it's time to put them into action.

Transform Your Customer Engagement with AI

Ready to transform your customer engagement with AI? This starter plan will guide you step-by-step through building more meaningful connections with your audience. Each step includes practical examples to help you get started, even if you're new to AI.

1. ***Collect Customer Feedback***
   Start by gathering insights from your customers. AI tools can analyze reviews, surveys, and social media interactions to uncover hidden patterns.
   ***Example**: Use a tool like **MonkeyLearn** to analyze product reviews. You might discover that customers love your product's design but frequently mention slow delivery times. These insights are invaluable for prioritizing improvements.*

2. ***Segment Your Customers***
   Group your customers into segments based on shared behaviors, demographics, or purchase history. AI tools can do this quickly and efficiently.
   ***Example**: With **HubSpot**, you can create a segment of customers who frequently shop during sales events. This allows you to tailor campaigns specifically to budget-conscious shoppers.*

3. ***Personalize Marketing Campaigns***
   *Craft customized messages for each segment to make your outreach more relevant and engaging. AI tools like **ChatGPT** can help create tailored content.*
   ***Example**: Send a personalized thank-you email to repeat customers, offering them a sneak peek at new products. This not only builds loyalty but also generates excitement for upcoming launches.*

4. ***Proactively Re-Engage Customers***
   Use AI to identify customers who haven't interacted with your brand in a while and create strategies to bring them back.
   ***Example**: With **Zoho CRM**, flag customers who haven't made a purchase in three months. Then, send them a special offer or a short survey to re-engage and learn why they've disengaged.*

5. ***Enhance Customer Service***
   Streamline your customer support with AI chatbots to handle FAQs while your team focuses on more complex issues.
   ***Example**: Implement an AI chatbot using **Intercom** to answer common questions about product returns. This ensures customers get quick responses while your team can concentrate on high-priority tasks.*

6. ***Track Engagement Metrics***
   Monitor key metrics like email open rates, click-through rates, and customer satisfaction scores. Use these insights to refine your strategies.
   ***Example**: With **Google Analytics**, track email campaign performance. You might find that personalized subject lines improve open rates by 20%, prompting you to apply this technique across all future campaigns.*

9.7 Summary

This chapter explored how AI revolutionizes customer engagement by enabling businesses to forge more profound, meaningful relationships with their customers. From uncovering hidden insights in customer feedback through sentiment analysis to crafting highly personalized interactions and delivering proactive engagement strategies, AI provides the tools to turn every customer touchpoint into a memorable experience. We also examined how data-driven strategies like customer segmentation and engagement tracking can refine your approach, ensuring your efforts resonate with your audience and drive loyalty.

By implementing these AI-driven strategies, you can transform your customer engagement efforts, making them more impactful, efficient, and customer-centric. The possibilities are vast, and the rewards go beyond financial gain—they strengthen the trust and loyalty that form the foundation of long-term business success.

Start small, focus on one touchpoint, and let AI help you create meaningful connections that keep your customers coming back.

But engagement is just one part of the equation. How do you ensure that your business operations align with larger goals like sustainability and ethical practices while maintaining profitability? In the next chapter, we'll delve into building a sustainable business with AI, exploring how this transformative technology can help your business thrive and positively impact the planet. Get ready to see how AI can be a powerful ally in creating a profitable and purposeful business.

Chapter 10: Building a Sustainable Business with AI

Practical Strategies for a Thriving, Responsible Business

Visualize this: You're running a quaint little café, the kind with mismatched chairs and the smell of fresh espresso wafting through the air. Business is booming, but you've noticed something—those adorable to-go cups are stacking up in the dumpster faster than you can say "triple-shot latte."

Enter AI, not just as the techy buzzword of the decade, but as your new eco-friendly sidekick ready to whip your operations into a sustainable shape. It's not about turning your café into a tech haven or having robots serve croissants (although, how cool would that be?).

Instead, it's about integrating AI in a way that's as smooth as your best flat white, prioritizing long-term health for both your business and the planet.

10.1 Energy-Efficient and Sustainable AI Solutions

Let's start with energy-efficient AI solutions, which are like swapping your old incandescent bulbs for snazzy LEDs. AI might get a bad rap for being an energy hog, but it can also be a force for good. Advanced algorithms now make AI systems more energy-efficient, optimizing their operations and reducing their carbon footprint.

It's like giving your business a green makeover without the need for solar panels on the roof. This means your operations can run as efficiently as a well-tuned espresso machine, cutting down on waste and conserving resources. AI-driven resource management systems take it a step further by smartly allocating resources, ensuring that nothing goes to waste—not even those precious coffee beans.

The Green Machine

AI isn't just about crunching numbers—it's your secret weapon for saving the planet. From cutting energy waste to optimizing resources, it's like having an eco-friendly superhero on your team.

Sustainable Supply Chain Management

Now, let's talk about supply chains, the lifeline of any business. Imagine your supply chain as a complex dance routine, where one misstep can send the whole performance tumbling. AI steps in as the choreographer, using predictive analytics for demand planning.

It's like having a crystal ball that sees when you'll need more milk or beans, ensuring you're never caught off guard. Real-time tracking further reduces waste by monitoring supply levels, adjusting orders as needed, and minimizing overproduction. This means fewer spoiled goods and more efficient use of resources.

By optimizing your supply chain, AI helps your business become leaner and greener, much like a well-pruned bonsai tree.

The Circular Economy and AI's Role

In the world of sustainability, the circular economy is the new cool kid on the block, and AI is its trusty sidekick. Think of it as a never-ending loop, where products are reused, recycled, and repurposed to minimize waste.

AI aids in recycling process optimization, ensuring materials are efficiently sorted and reused. It's like having a super-efficient recycling bin that knows exactly where everything goes. Product lifecycle management with AI insights is another game changer, providing data on how products are used and when they need replacing.

This knowledge allows businesses to design products that last longer and are easier to recycle, closing the loop and reducing environmental impact.

AI's Role in Sustainable Success

Consider apparel brands that have adopted AI to reduce waste. They utilize AI to analyze fashion trends, predicting demand with precision and ensuring that production aligns with market needs. This means fewer unsold items languishing in warehouses, reducing both waste and costs.

Meanwhile, tech firms are utilizing AI to optimize energy use in data centers. By analyzing energy consumption patterns, AI suggests adjustments that reduce power usage while maintaining performance. These companies showcase how AI can drive sustainability, proving it's not just a buzzword but a practical solution for real-world challenges.

Incorporating AI for sustainable growth involves making informed choices that benefit both your business and the environment. It's not about sacrificing profits for the planet but finding that sweet spot where both thrive.

Whether you're running a charming café or a bustling tech firm, AI offers tools to streamline operations, reduce waste, and promote sustainability. As we continue, consider how these strategies can be applied to your business, transforming challenges into opportunities for growth and innovation.

10.2 Aligning AI with Business Ethics

Imagine AI as your trusty assistant, helping you make decisions faster than a barista can whip up a cappuccino. But with great power comes great responsibility—cue the ethics talk.

You see, using AI in business isn't just about getting the job done; it's also about doing it right. Transparency in AI decision-making is crucial. Think of it as showing your math work in school. When AI makes a decision, it should be clear and understandable, not a mysterious black box that spits out solutions. Customers and stakeholders need to see the process, ensuring that decisions are based on fair and unbiased data.

The next piece of the puzzle is fairness in AI-driven outcomes. It's about ensuring that AI doesn't play favorites and treats everyone equally, like a judge who's never had a bad day. This means designing systems that provide equal opportunities and access, regardless of who's on the receiving end.

Implementing Ethical Oversight

Now, let's talk about implementing these ethical principles. Start by setting up ethical review boards for AI projects. Imagine them as referees in a game, ensuring everyone plays by the rules. These boards evaluate AI systems, keeping an eye out for any ethical red flags.

They're the guardians of fairness and transparency, making sure AI aligns with your company's values and ethical standards. Establishing clear accountability structures is also key. Picture it as a game of tag, where everyone knows who's "it."

When AI goes awry, accountability structures ensure there's a clear path to address and fix issues. This means assigning roles and responsibilities so everyone knows who monitors and maintains ethical standards. It's like having a safety net under your AI trapeze, ensuring that even if things go south, there's a plan in place to catch and correct them.

Addressing AI Bias and Discrimination

Addressing AI bias and discrimination is like cleaning out your closet—necessary but sometimes uncomfortable. Regular bias audits in AI algorithms are essential. They're like spring cleaning, keeping your AI systems fresh and free of hidden biases. These audits check for any disparities in how AI treats different groups, ensuring fairness and equity.

Training data diversity checks are another tool in your ethical arsenal. It's like making sure your movie collection isn't all rom-coms; you need variety. By using diverse data sets, you ensure that AI learns from a wide range of experiences and perspectives, reducing the risk of bias and discrimination.

This diversity strengthens your AI, making it more robust and inclusive.

Examples of Ethical AI Practices

Let's spotlight some real-world examples of ethical AI practices. In the financial services industry, companies are using AI to ensure fairness in credit scoring. It's like having a transparent grading system where everyone knows the criteria. By analyzing data and adjusting algorithms, they ensure credit decisions are based on accurate and unbiased information.

Building a Sustainable Business with AI

Objective*: Leverage AI tools and strategies to create a business that balances profitability with sustainability and ethical practices.*

Steps*:*

1. ***Identify Sustainability Challenges****: Evaluate your business operations to identify inefficiencies or areas with environmental impact (e.g., energy use, waste, or logistics).*
   Example*: "What are the most common sustainability challenges faced by small e-commerce businesses?"*

2. ***Choose AI Tools to Address Chal****lenges: Select AI solutions tailored to your specific needs, such as optimizing energy consumption or supply chain logistics.*
   Example*: "Recommend AI tools to reduce energy consumption in a small manufacturing plant."*

3. ***Monitor and Measure Impact****: Use AI-powered analytics tools to track key sustainability metrics like carbon footprint, energy usage, or waste reduction.*
   Example*: "How can AI help measure the environmental impact of packaging choices?"*

4. ***Refine Operations with Data Insights****: Continuously improve processes by analyzing data and identifying opportunities for further optimization.*
   Example*: "Suggest ways to use AI to optimize a supply chain for sustainability."*

5. ***Align Practices with Ethical Standards****: Ensure that AI implementations respect ethical considerations, such as data privacy and fairness.*
   Example*: "What ethical guidelines should I follow when using AI in customer-facing applications?"*

6. ***Scale and Share Success****: Expand successful sustainable practices to other parts of your business and communicate your efforts to stakeholders.*
   Example*: "Draft a message to share our sustainability achievements with customers."*

In healthcare, providers are leveraging AI for equitable patient care. Imagine an AI-powered doctor's assistant that treats every patient with the same level of care and attention. By addressing potential biases in diagnostic algorithms, healthcare providers ensure AI serves all patients equally, improving outcomes and building trust.

These examples show that ethical AI isn't just a theory; it's a practice that companies are implementing to make a real difference.

10.3 Long-Term Planning with AI

Think of AI as your business's crystal ball—not one that tells you the winning lottery numbers, but one that provides insights into the future of your operations. Incorporating AI into long-term strategies involves more than just a sprinkle of technology magic; it's about weaving AI into the very fabric of your business planning.

AI-Driven Scenario Planning

AI-driven scenario planning is like having a GPS that not only shows you the route but also forecasts traffic jams and suggests detours. By simulating various business scenarios, AI enables you to anticipate potential challenges and opportunities, thereby preparing you for different outcomes.

Strategic foresight, leveraging AI predictions, is another key advantage. By analyzing vast amounts of data, AI can predict trends and guide your strategic decisions, much like a wise old mentor whispering the secrets of the market into your ear.

Predictive Risk Analytics and Disaster Recovery

Risk management is a bit like preparing for a camping trip. You've checked the weather, packed extra socks, and have a map ready. But wouldn't it be better if you had a guide who knew the terrain? That's where AI steps in.

Predictive risk analytics are the tools you need to navigate the unpredictable landscape of business. AI identifies potential risks before they become real problems, allowing you to take proactive measures. Whether it's a market shift or supply chain disruption, AI equips you with the knowledge to tackle risks head-on.

When it comes to disaster recovery planning, AI is your safety net. It helps create robust contingency plans, ensuring that your business can bounce back from any setback, like a well-prepared scout ready to face the wilderness.

Innovation Roadmaps and Product Development Timelines

A roadmap is more than just a piece of paper with lines on it; it's your guide to the future. Developing AI-driven innovation roadmaps ensures your business remains on the cutting edge. Start by identifying AI opportunities in R&D. Think of it as prospecting for gold, where each nugget represents a potential breakthrough.

Whether it's enhancing existing products or developing new ones, AI can streamline your R&D process, making it more efficient and effective. AI-enhanced product development timelines are like having a time machine, allowing you to see the future of your product lineup. By integrating AI into the development process, you can accelerate timelines and bring innovations to market faster than your competitors, ensuring you're always ahead of the curve.

Real-World Examples of AI in Long-Term Strategy

Let's look at some real-world examples of businesses that have successfully integrated AI into their long-term strategies. In the automotive industry, companies are leveraging AI for autonomous vehicle development. Imagine cars that can drive themselves, navigating the complexities of traffic with ease. AI plays a crucial role in this transformation, analyzing data from sensors to improve navigation and safety features.

Meanwhile, in the retail sector, companies are using AI for long-term customer engagement strategies. By analyzing purchase data and customer interactions, AI helps retailers create personalized experiences that build loyalty and drive repeat business.

These examples illustrate how AI is not just a tool but a strategic partner, helping businesses navigate the future with confidence and precision.

Incorporating AI into long-term planning might seem like a daunting task, but it's an investment worth making. From scenario planning to risk management and innovation roadmaps, AI offers a treasure trove of tools to help your business thrive. It's about seeing the bigger picture, understanding the trends, and being ready for whatever the future holds. Whether you're in tech, retail, or any other industry, AI's insights and predictions can guide your business into a prosperous future, ensuring you're always ready for the next big thing.

10.4 Balancing Profit and Sustainability

Picture yourself in a bustling café, where the aroma of roasted beans mingles with the chatter of satisfied customers. Now imagine that each cup you serve isn't just a source of joy but a testament to sustainable practices that drive profitability. That's the magic of sustainable AI. It's about making good choices for the planet and your pocket.

Energy-Efficient AI Operations

Energy-efficient AI operations are like swapping your café's incandescent bulbs for LEDs, saving on energy bills while reducing your carbon footprint. These systems optimize energy use, ensuring your business runs smoothly without guzzling power.

It's like having a barista who never spills a drop or wastes a bean, making every operation as lean as a well-pulled espresso shot.

Sustainable Product Offerings

Sustainable product offerings can also boost revenue. Imagine your café introducing a line of eco-friendly mugs that not only delight customers but also encourage them to think green.

When AI helps design these products, using minimal resources and maximizing appeal, your business stands out. Customers today are drawn to brands that prioritize sustainability. By embracing AI to develop such offerings, you tap into a market eager for products that reflect their values.

It's like offering a menu item that not only tastes good but feels good, resonating with the eco-conscious customer who wants to make a difference with every purchase.

Business Models That Merge Profit and Sustainability

Let's talk about business models that marry profit with sustainability. AI-driven subscription models are like having a steady stream of regulars who never miss their morning brew, ensuring consistent revenue.

These models optimize resource use, tailoring services to meet customer needs without excess. Imagine a subscription coffee service that delivers exactly the right amount of beans each month, reducing waste and satisfying demand.

Then there are sharing economy platforms, enhanced by AI analytics, that maximize resource utilization. Think of it as a community tool library where everyone borrows what they need, minimizing individual consumption.

AI analyzes usage patterns, ensuring resources are shared efficiently, much like a perfectly coordinated potluck where nothing goes to waste.

Reducing Waste and Optimizing Transportation

In the food industry, AI forecasting reduces waste by predicting demand with precision. Imagine your café knowing exactly how many croissants to bake each day, ensuring freshness without leftovers.

This reduces waste and optimizes ingredient use, translating to cost savings and higher profits. AI's route optimization in transportation is like finding the fastest path through the morning rush to deliver your pastries warm and on time.

By minimizing emissions and fuel use, these optimizations not only cut costs but also demonstrate your commitment to sustainability, appealing to customers who value eco-friendly practices.

Tracking Sustainability Metrics

Tracking sustainability metrics is crucial for maintaining balance. AI-powered sustainability scorecards provide insights into your business's environmental impact, much like a fitness tracker that monitors your health.

These scorecards offer a clear picture of energy use, waste reduction, and other key metrics. Integrated reporting of financial and environmental KPIs ensures you stay on track, balancing profit with planet-friendly practices.

It's like having a dashboard that shows not just your car's speed but also its fuel efficiency, giving you a comprehensive view of performance. By monitoring these metrics, you can make informed decisions that sustain your business's growth while preserving the environment.

Finding Your Sustainability Sweet Spot

***Objective**: Identify actionable opportunities to align profitability and sustainability in your business using AI.*

***Steps**:*

1. ***Reflect on Your Current Practices**: List three areas in your business that have potential for improvement in sustainability or ethical practices. These could include energy use, supply chain efficiency, waste management, or employee well-being.*
   ***Example**: Packaging materials, delivery routes, and employee training.*

2. ***Explore AI Solutions**: Research or brainstorm how AI could address these areas. Use tools like ChatGPT to simulate ideas or identify technologies that could make an impact.*
   ***Example**: "How can AI help optimize delivery routes to reduce fuel consumption?"*

3. ***Weigh Profitability and Sustainability**: For each area, consider how implementing AI solutions could affect both sustainability and profitability.*
   - *Will it reduce costs or increase efficiency?*
   - *Will it enhance your reputation with eco-conscious customers?*
   - *Could it have an upfront cost that pays off over time?*

4. ***Plan Your First Step**: Choose one area to focus on and outline the first action you'll take to implement an AI-driven solution.*
   ***Example**: Switching to AI-optimized delivery routes to save on fuel and reduce emissions*

5. ***Measure and Adjust**: Define how you'll measure success. What metrics will you track to ensure the change is both profitable and sustainable?*
   ***Example**: Carbon emissions saved, fuel costs reduced, or customer feedback on sustainability initiatives.*

10.5 Future-Proofing Your Business with AI

Picture your business as a sleek, modern ship sailing across an ocean of opportunity. To keep it on course, you need to stay ahead of emerging AI trends.

Embracing Emerging AI Trends

One such trend is quantum computing, which promises to turbocharge AI capabilities by processing data at unprecedented speeds. Imagine solving complex problems in seconds rather than hours.

This technology could revolutionize everything from logistics to healthcare, offering insights and solutions previously thought impossible.

Then there's AI-driven edge computing, which brings processing power closer to the data source. Think of it as moving the brain closer to the fingertips, allowing for faster, more efficient data handling.

This is particularly useful for businesses needing real-time processing, such as in autonomous vehicles or smart home technologies. By understanding these trends, you position your business to leverage cutting-edge tools, ensuring you're not just reacting to changes but leading them.

Navigating AI Regulations

Navigating the shifting sands of AI regulations can feel like trying to dance on a moving carpet. Laws evolve, and staying compliant is crucial.

Start by understanding data protection laws, which safeguard consumer privacy and dictate how data is collected, stored, and used. Compliance ensures you're not caught off guard by hefty fines or legal challenges.

Monitoring AI ethics regulations is equally important. These guidelines ensure AI systems operate fairly and transparently, aligning with societal values and expectations. It's like having a rulebook that keeps everyone on the same page.

By keeping tabs on these regulations, you not only protect your business but also build trust with your customers, who appreciate transparency and ethical practices. This proactive approach ensures your business remains agile and adaptable, ready to meet any regulatory challenge head-on.

Cultivating an Adaptable AI Strategy

To future-proof your business, cultivate an adaptable AI strategy. Flexibility is key. Continuous learning and adaptation in AI systems mean you're always at the forefront of innovation.

It's like having a dynamic roadmap that adjusts with every twist and turn. Encourage your team to embrace lifelong learning, exploring new AI tools and techniques that enhance business operations.

Agile AI project management frameworks support this adaptability by promoting iterative development and rapid response to change. It's a bit like having a Swiss Army knife for project management—tools and processes that evolve with your needs.

This approach not only keeps your business nimble but also fosters a culture of innovation, where ideas and creativity thrive.

Examples of Future-Proofing Success

Let's look at some examples of businesses that have effectively prepared for AI-driven futures. Tech startups are pioneering AI-based cybersecurity, developing systems that detect and neutralize threats in real-time. Imagine a digital fortress that adapts to ever-changing threats, protecting valuable information from cybercriminals.

Meanwhile, energy companies are exploring AI for renewable energy management. By analyzing data from solar panels and wind turbines, AI optimizes energy production and storage, ensuring maximum efficiency and minimal waste.

These businesses are not just surviving but thriving, using AI to carve out new paths in their respective industries.

As you integrate AI into your business, remember that future-proofing is about more than just adopting the latest technology. It's about building a resilient strategy that embraces change and leverages AI's full potential.

By staying informed of emerging trends, complying with regulations, and cultivating adaptability, you ensure your business is ready for whatever the future holds. With AI as your ally, you're equipped to navigate the complexities of the modern business landscape, turning challenges into opportunities for growth and success.

10.6 Summary

In this chapter, we explored how AI can help businesses balance profitability and sustainability, paving the way for long-term success. From energy-efficient operations to sustainable supply chain management, AI offers practical tools to reduce waste, optimize resources, and foster environmental stewardship. We also discussed the importance of ethical AI practices, emphasizing fairness, transparency, and inclusivity in decision-making. By incorporating AI-driven long-term planning and predictive analytics, businesses can not only prepare for challenges but also seize opportunities for innovation and growth.

As we've seen, AI has the potential to align business goals with broader societal values, proving that profitability and sustainability can coexist. But what does this look like in practice? How are companies across industries using AI to solve real-world challenges and achieve meaningful impact?

In the next chapter, we'll dive into case studies and success stories that bring these concepts to life, showcasing how businesses of all sizes are harnessing AI to drive innovation and transform their operations. You'll see the remarkable ways AI is shaping the future from retail to healthcare to logistics. Let's turn theory into action and explore the real-world power of AI.

Chapter 11: Case Studies and Real-World Applications

Unlocking Success Stories and Practical Lessons from AI Pioneers

Artificial Intelligence is more than just a concept; it's a force that's reshaping businesses across industries. But what does AI look like in the real world? This chapter takes you on a journey through diverse case studies, showcasing how businesses—big and small—are using AI to solve problems, innovate, and thrive.

Whether it's a bustling bakery using AI to predict demand, a boutique leveraging chatbots for personalized service, or an art studio embracing AI to enhance creativity, these stories highlight the tangible impact AI can have. Along the way, we'll explore not just the successes but also the challenges these businesses faced and the lessons they learned.

This chapter is about bringing theory to life. It's about understanding how AI operates in the trenches and how you can draw inspiration from these examples to apply AI in your own business. Let's dive into these snapshots of AI in action and uncover the strategies and takeaways that can help you make the most of this transformative technology.

11.1 AI in Inventory Management: The Bakery

A local bakery is more than a place to buy bread; it's a community hub, a cornerstone of comfort and familiarity. For Sarah, the owner of such a bakery, managing inventory was a constant challenge. Some days, her shelves overflowed with unsold baguettes, while on others, customers left disappointed when their favorites sold out by noon.

By integrating AI into her operations, Sarah found a solution that transformed her business. AI-powered inventory management systems analyzed historical sales data, local events, weather patterns, and more to accurately predict demand. The result? Sarah was able to bake smarter, reducing waste and ensuring her customers could always find what they wanted.

This wasn't just about solving an inventory problem—it was about building trust with her customers. Consistently having fresh, perfectly baked goods on hand kept her customers coming back and created a ripple effect of goodwill throughout the community.

Lessons from the Bakery

1. **Understanding Demand:** AI analyzes multiple factors, such as customer preferences, seasonal trends, and external influences, to provide actionable insights.

2. **Reducing Waste:** Smarter inventory management minimizes overproduction, saving costs and supporting sustainability.

3. **Enhancing Customer Loyalty:** Consistently meeting customer expectations strengthens relationships and encourages repeat business.

Could a similar AI approach streamline inventory management in your business? Think about the factors that drive demand in your operations and consider how AI could help you predict and meet those needs.

11.2 Personalization with Chatbots: The Boutique

Mike's corner boutique is a treasure trove of unique trinkets and handmade crafts, but like many small business owners, he faced an uphill battle against online giants. His customers loved the charm and character of his store, but his online presence wasn't converting casual visitors into loyal customers.

Enter AI-powered chatbots. Mike integrated these virtual assistants into his website to recreate the personalized in-store experience online. Chatbots welcomed visitors, answered their questions, recommended products based on browsing history, and even infused conversations with a touch of humor.

The impact was immediate. Customer engagement soared as visitors felt attended to, much like they would in the boutique itself. The chatbots not only helped customers find what they needed but also suggested complementary items, subtly boosting sales. For Mike, the chatbots became indispensable team members, working 24/7 to create a seamless shopping experience.

Lessons from the Boutique

1. **Enhanced Customer Experience:** Chatbots mimic personalized service, making online interactions feel warm and engaging.
2. **Boosted Sales:** AI recommendations increase average purchase values by highlighting complementary products.
3. **Round-the-Clock Support:** Unlike human employees, chatbots work tirelessly, ensuring customers are always supported.

What could a chatbot do for your business? Think about your customers' most common questions or needs and how an AI-powered assistant might help meet them effectively.

11.3 Cost Savings through Automation: The Small Office

Running a small office often means juggling tight budgets and limited resources. For one small team, finding ways to save money without sacrificing quality was a constant challenge. Enter AI-powered automation, a solution that streamlined their operations and significantly reduced costs.

Energy Management: The office installed an AI-driven energy management system. This tool optimized energy usage, adjusting lighting and temperature settings based on occupancy and time of day. It was like having an energy-saving expert on call, ensuring no watt was wasted.

Automated Accounting: AI also took over tedious tasks like data entry and invoice categorization. By automating these processes, the team reduced errors and freed up time for more strategic work. Instead of spending hours on spreadsheets, the office staff focused on projects that drove growth and innovation.

The results spoke volumes. Energy costs dropped by 20%, and administrative efficiency soared. The team reinvested their savings into employee development and client acquisition, transforming the office into a lean, productive powerhouse.

Lessons from the Small Office

1. **Operational Efficiency:** Automation eliminates time-consuming manual tasks, increasing productivity.

2. **Cost Savings:** AI systems optimize resource usage, reducing unnecessary expenses.
3. **Scalability:** Automated tools grow with your business, adapting to increased demands without significant additional costs.

Think about your business operations. Which tasks could be automated to save time and reduce costs?

11.4 Personalized Experiences: The Bookstore Example

Imagine stepping into a cozy bookstore filled with the scent of fresh coffee and the promise of literary treasures. For one independent bookstore, creating personalized experiences was key to standing out from larger competitors. AI became their secret weapon in turning occasional visitors into loyal customers.

AI-Driven Recommendations: The store implemented a recommendation engine powered by AI. Based on past purchases and browsing behavior, it suggested new titles that matched customers' preferences. It was like having a well-read friend guiding each shopper to their next favorite book.

Loyalty Programs: The bookstore also introduced an AI-enhanced loyalty program. By analyzing purchasing patterns, the system personalized rewards and incentives. Frequent mystery buyers received discounts on thrillers, while poetry lovers were offered early access to exclusive collections.

In-Store and Online Integration: The bookstore bridged the gap between physical and digital spaces. In-store, an AI-powered kiosk provided recommendations and allowed customers to check availability. Online, the same AI system delivered personalized emails and promotions, keeping customers engaged between visits.

The results? Sales increased by 30%, and customer retention rates soared. The bookstore became a beloved community hub, combining the charm of a local business with the sophistication of AI-driven personalization.

Key Takeaways for Personalized Experiences

1. **Enhanced Engagement:** AI helps tailor experiences, making customers feel understood and valued.

2. **Hybrid Integration:** AI can connect in-store and online interactions, creating seamless customer journeys.
3. **Customer Loyalty:** Personalized rewards and communications build lasting relationships.

Could AI personalization help your business create memorable customer experiences?

11.5 Creative Innovation with AI: The Art Studio and Restaurant

AI is not just a tool for efficiency; it's a partner in creative expression. In the worlds of art and cuisine, AI is sparking innovation and pushing boundaries, allowing creators to explore new horizons.

Art Studio Transformation:
In one small art studio, AI became the collaborator every artist dreams of. Using AI tools, the studio created stunning digital artworks that blended traditional techniques with cutting-edge algorithms. These tools analyzed historical art styles and suggested new combinations of colors, textures, and patterns, inspiring fresh creations.

For example, one artist used AI to generate unique abstract backgrounds for paintings, which were then completed by hand. The result was a series of pieces that felt both modern and timeless, captivating collectors and gallery audiences alike.

Culinary Creativity in Restaurants:
Over in a trendy urban restaurant, the head chef partnered with AI to innovate menu offerings. By analyzing flavor profiles, dietary trends, and seasonal ingredients, the AI suggested combinations that were both surprising and delightful.

One standout dish combined an unexpected blend of herbs and spices that became an instant hit. The AI didn't replace the chef's creativity—it augmented it, providing insights and suggestions the chef might not have considered on their own.

The Results:
Both businesses saw increased customer interest and revenue. The art studio expanded its portfolio with digital collections, reaching new audiences online. The restaurant gained a reputation for bold, inventive dishes that kept diners coming back for more.

Key Takeaways for Creative Innovation

1. **Inspiration Amplified:** AI doesn't replace creativity; it enhances it by offering new perspectives and ideas.
2. **Market Expansion:** AI-enabled innovations can attract new audiences and create fresh opportunities for growth.
3. **Collaboration, Not Competition:** AI works as a creative partner, supporting human ingenuity.

How might AI enhance the creative processes in your business?

11.6 AI Transformations in Diverse Industries

AI's impact spans across a variety of industries, revolutionizing operations, enhancing efficiency, and opening new avenues for growth. Let's explore some transformative examples.

Manufacturing and Predictive Maintenance

In manufacturing, AI acts as the ultimate foreman, ensuring machinery runs smoothly and efficiently. Predictive maintenance systems use AI to monitor equipment performance, detecting early signs of wear and tear.

For instance, a factory integrated AI sensors into its production line, which identified potential malfunctions before they caused downtime. This proactive approach saved thousands of dollars in repair costs and avoided disruptions to production schedules.

Key Benefit: Predictive maintenance reduces costs and improves reliability, ensuring a seamless manufacturing process.

Agriculture and Precision Farming

AI is also reshaping agriculture through precision farming. Drones equipped with AI scan fields to gather data on soil quality, moisture levels, and crop health.

One farmer used this technology to optimize irrigation, ensuring water was distributed precisely where it was needed. The result? Increased crop yield and reduced water consumption contribute to sustainable farming practices.

Key Benefit: AI allows farmers to work smarter, conserving resources while maximizing productivity.

Service Industries and Enhanced Customer Experiences

AI is making its mark in service industries, elevating customer satisfaction. Hotels use AI-powered systems for seamless check-ins and personalized guest experiences.

Imagine arriving at a hotel where the AI knows your room preferences and suggests local attractions based on your previous visits. This level of personalization fosters loyalty and enhances the guest experience.

Key Benefit: AI ensures tailored, memorable customer experiences, driving repeat business.

Healthcare and Diagnostic Tools

In healthcare, AI acts as a vital assistant to doctors and medical staff. Diagnostic tools analyze medical data, providing faster and more accurate assessments.

For example, an AI system flagged early signs of a serious condition in a patient's test results, enabling timely intervention and potentially saving a life.

Key Benefit: AI improves accuracy and efficiency in medical diagnoses, contributing to better patient outcomes.

Environmental Sustainability and Waste Reduction

AI supports sustainability efforts by optimizing waste management and energy use.

One waste management company implemented AI sorting systems to identify recyclables more effectively. Meanwhile, smart grids powered by AI balanced energy distribution, reducing overall consumption.

Key Benefit: AI promotes sustainable practices, helping businesses reduce their environmental impact.

Summary of Transformations Across Industries

From manufacturing to healthcare, AI is driving efficiency and innovation. By leveraging AI, businesses can reduce costs, improve accuracy, and create tailored experiences for their customers.

11.7 Overcoming Challenges with AI

While the benefits of AI are clear, integrating it into your business can come with challenges. Addressing these obstacles head-on ensures a smoother journey toward AI adoption.

Data Privacy Concerns and Cost Challenges

One of the biggest hurdles for businesses is maintaining data privacy. Using AI requires handling sensitive customer information, and businesses must strike a balance between innovation and security.

A small financial firm implemented AI to analyze customer transactions but faced concerns about protecting sensitive data. By adopting encryption and secure storage methods, they ensured compliance with privacy regulations while harnessing AI's capabilities.

Key Insight: Transparent practices and robust security measures build trust and safeguard sensitive data.

Cost can also be a barrier. The initial investment in AI tools or platforms may seem daunting, especially for small businesses.

However, businesses can start small by adopting cost-effective, scalable cloud-based AI solutions. For instance, an e-commerce store used an AI chatbot service that offered a pay-as-you-go pricing model, reducing upfront costs while improving customer support.

Key Insight: Scalable solutions and cloud-based tools make AI accessible, even for businesses with tight budgets.

Building Cross-Functional Teams and Collaboration

Successful AI implementation is rarely a one-person effort. It requires collaboration across departments to ensure seamless integration.

A retail chain created a cross-functional team of IT specialists, marketing professionals, and operations managers to implement AI-powered inventory management. This diverse expertise ensured the system met the company's technical and business needs.

Key Insight: Cross-functional teams enable well-rounded AI adoption that aligns with business objectives.

Learning from Real-World Resilience

Businesses that adapt quickly can overcome AI-related hurdles.

A logistics company faced major disruptions during a global crisis. By adopting AI forecasting tools, they optimized routes and ensured timely deliveries despite supply chain challenges.

Another business used AI for compliance, reducing regulatory risks and avoiding costly penalties. These proactive measures allowed them to navigate challenges and emerge stronger.

Key Insight: Resilience and adaptability are key to thriving with AI, even in uncertain conditions.

Lessons from Failed Implementations

Not every AI story is one of success. Businesses that lack clear objectives or fail to train employees on new systems often struggle to see results.

A small manufacturer invested in predictive analytics without setting clear goals. As a result, the system delivered data, but the business lacked direction on how to act on it.

Key Insight: Define objectives and KPIs before implementation to ensure measurable success.

Continuous Training and Support

AI isn't a one-and-done solution. It requires ongoing maintenance and adaptation to remain effective.

A marketing agency invested in continuous training, ensuring their team stayed updated on the latest AI trends. This commitment allowed them to extract more value from their tools and adapt to changing customer needs.

Key Insight: Continuous learning ensures AI systems remain relevant and effective over time.

11.8 Lessons Learned from AI Pioneers

The journey of successful AI adoption is paved with insights from those who have navigated it before. By studying these pioneers, businesses can extract valuable lessons to guide their own strategies.

Learning from the Giants: Tech Titans as AI Trailblazers

Tech giants like Google and Amazon have redefined what's possible with AI. These companies invest heavily in research and development, creating groundbreaking technologies that reshape industries.

For example, Amazon's AI-driven recommendation engine not only enhances customer experience but also generates significant revenue by increasing average purchase sizes. Google, on the other hand, has leveraged AI to improve search algorithms and power voice recognition systems, setting new benchmarks for usability and innovation.

Key Insight: Investing in R&D and continuously iterating on AI tools can yield transformative results.

Small and Mighty: Startups Disrupting with AI

Startups are using AI to challenge industry norms, proving that innovation isn't limited to big players.

For instance, a small healthcare startup developed an AI-driven platform for personalized fitness plans, filling a niche that larger companies had overlooked. By focusing on a specific market segment and leveraging AI, they quickly gained a competitive edge.

Key Insight: Niche markets offer opportunities for smaller businesses to thrive with targeted AI applications.

Cultivating an AI-Driven Culture: Fostering Innovation and Experimentation

A critical factor in AI success is the culture that surrounds its implementation. Companies that foster creativity and encourage experimentation are better positioned to harness AI's potential.

A mid-sized software company implemented an "innovation lab" where employees could experiment with AI tools to solve real business challenges. This initiative resulted in several successful projects, including an AI-powered support bot that reduced customer service costs by 30%.

Key Insight: Encourage experimentation and provide employees with the tools to innovate without fear of failure.

Education as the Lifeblood of AI Success

Ongoing education ensures teams remain equipped to adapt to evolving AI tools and methodologies.

A manufacturing company partnered with local universities to offer AI training programs for its employees. This not only upskilled their workforce but also fostered loyalty and engagement among staff.

Key Insight: Invest in employee education to build a knowledgeable team that can effectively leverage AI.

Strategic Partnerships: Collaborating for AI Excellence

Collaboration with external partners accelerates AI adoption and innovation.

A financial services firm partnered with an AI research lab to co-develop predictive analytics tools. This collaboration enabled the firm to offer groundbreaking services that competitors couldn't match.

Key Insight: Partnerships can provide access to expertise and resources that enhance AI implementation.

11.9 Applying AI Insights to Your Business

Turning insights into actionable strategies is the final step in making AI work for your business. This section focuses on how to adapt AI success stories to your unique needs, structure an effective implementation plan, and foster a culture of continuous learning.

Adapting AI Strategies to Fit Your Business Needs

The power of AI lies in its flexibility, but implementing it effectively requires thoughtful customization.

For instance, a small retail business can learn from larger retailers' AI-powered inventory systems by scaling the technology to match their resources. Instead of investing in enterprise-level software, they might use affordable cloud-based AI tools to track stock levels and predict demand.

Action Tip: Identify AI strategies in industries similar to yours and adapt them to fit your budget, resources, and goals.

Structuring an Effective AI Implementation Plan

A well-structured plan ensures a smooth AI adoption process. Start by clearly defining your objectives.

For example, if your goal is to enhance customer engagement, outline specific metrics, such as increased email open rates or reduced response times. Use these goals to guide your choice of AI tools and integration timeline.

Action Tip: Break your implementation into phases, testing and refining each step before scaling. This reduces risk and ensures measurable success.

Embracing Continuous Learning and Evaluation

AI is a dynamic field, and staying relevant requires ongoing adaptation.

Regularly reviewing AI performance helps identify areas for improvement. For example, a company using an AI chatbot might monitor response times and customer satisfaction scores to refine the bot's functionality. This iterative approach ensures the technology evolves with your business needs.

Action Tip: Schedule periodic evaluations of your AI systems, using feedback from employees and customers to guide improvements.

Reflection Section: Your AI Action Plan

Take a moment to outline how AI can support your business.

1. Identify three areas where AI could address challenges or enhance operations.
2. Research AI tools that align with these needs.
3. Draft a phased timeline for implementation, starting with small-scale projects.

Pro Tip: Use this reflection as a foundation for crafting a detailed AI strategy.

11.10 Summary

This chapter has shown the remarkable breadth of AI's applications, from streamlining operations and enhancing customer experiences to enabling creativity and innovation. Through real-world examples and actionable strategies, we've explored how AI is not just a tool but a transformative partner in building a thriving business.

Key takeaways include:

- **AI's flexibility and scalability:** Whether you're a small boutique or a global enterprise, AI can be tailored to meet your specific needs.
- **The importance of strategy:** A clear, structured implementation plan is essential to achieving measurable success.
- **Continuous learning:** AI is not a one-time solution but an evolving tool that grows with your business.

As you integrate AI into your operations, remember that success is a journey, not a destination. Every step, from small experiments to larger-scale adoption, builds your capacity to innovate and adapt in an ever-changing business landscape.

But what about the challenges that come with implementing AI? How do businesses navigate ethical considerations, data privacy concerns, and the need for cross-functional collaboration?

In the next chapter, we'll tackle these topics head-on, exploring the complexities of AI adoption and providing strategies to overcome obstacles. Together, we'll ensure your AI journey is as smooth and impactful as possible. Let's dive into the practicalities of making AI work for you in the real world.

Chapter 12: Building Trust with AI

How Ethics, Transparency, and Accountability Create Long-Term Success

Trust is the foundation of every successful AI-driven business. In recent years, the conversation about AI ethics has shifted from broad principles to enforceable law. The EU AI Act (enforced in 2025) introduced risk-based categories for AI systems, transparency obligations, and disclosure requirements when users interact with AI. Similar frameworks are emerging in the U.S., Canada, and Asia, emphasizing fairness, accountability, and data traceability.

For entrepreneurs, this means that ethical AI isn't just good practice—it's compliance. Building trustworthy systems now involves documenting how data flows through your tools, validating outputs, and providing transparency to both customers and regulators.

12.1 The Role of Ethics in AI

Ethics is the cornerstone of trust in AI, shaping how systems operate and how they impact society. In the realm of AI, ethics ensures that decisions are not just efficient but also fair, transparent, and aligned with human values.

Transparency is a key principle. It means AI systems should operate like a clear window, allowing users to see and understand how decisions are made. Without transparency, algorithms can feel like black boxes, leaving users skeptical of their outcomes.

Accountability is another critical pillar. When AI systems make decisions, someone must take responsibility. Whether it's a developer, business owner, or even a broader team, accountability ensures there's a clear line of oversight. This is essential for building trust and providing recourse when things go wrong.

Ultimately, ethical AI is about balance. It involves fostering innovation while ensuring systems operate within a framework of trust, respect, and responsibility.

The AI Compass

Ethics is your compass in the AI wilderness. Without it, you risk getting lost in the fog of innovation—so keep it handy to navigate the right path.

12.2 Accountability and Transparency in AI

Accountability and transparency are two sides of the same coin in ethical AI. While accountability ensures someone takes responsibility for AI-driven decisions, transparency ensures users understand how those decisions are made. Together, they build trust, mitigate risks, and foster confidence in AI systems.

Defining Accountability

Accountability in AI involves clearly identifying who is responsible for the outcomes of AI-driven actions. For example, if a customer service chatbot provides incorrect information, it's crucial for users to know how to escalate their concerns to a human representative.

To establish accountability:

1. **Define Roles and Responsibilities**: Developers must create ethical and technically sound systems, while business leaders must oversee their alignment with company values.

2. **Create Remedy Mechanisms**: Offer clear channels for users to report and resolve issues, ensuring a swift and transparent response.

Case in Action

In the healthcare industry, AI diagnostic tools assist doctors, but ultimate accountability remains with the physician. This blend of human oversight and AI-driven efficiency highlights a balanced approach to accountability.

Promoting Transparency

Transparency ensures that AI systems operate openly, avoiding the "black box" problem where decisions seem mysterious or arbitrary.

To foster transparency:

1. **Explain AI Decisions Clearly**: Provide users with understandable reasons for AI actions. For example, a loan application might be rejected due to "low credit score" rather than vague or technical explanations.

2. **Implement Accessible Systems**: Use plain language and user-friendly interfaces to make AI comprehensible, even for non-technical audiences.

Case in Action

Financial institutions now share credit scoring criteria with customers, helping them understand how decisions were made and how they can improve outcomes in the future.

Building Trust through Accountability and Transparency

When users see how AI decisions are made and know who to contact for support, they're more likely to trust the system. Together, these principles create an ethical foundation that ensures AI systems serve their intended purpose while respecting user needs and expectations.

12.3 Creating Ethical AI Policies

Establishing ethical AI policies is essential for businesses that want to integrate AI responsibly while building trust with customers and stakeholders. These policies serve as a roadmap, ensuring that AI systems align with your organization's values and operate transparently, fairly, and securely.

Defining Core Ethical Standards

Creating effective policies starts with defining your organization's core ethical principles. These standards should reflect your business's values and priorities, whether it's fairness, transparency, or inclusivity. Think of these principles as the foundation of your AI framework—they guide every decision and action.

For example, a small e-commerce business might define ethical standards around customer data usage, ensuring data is collected only with explicit consent and used solely to enhance the shopping experience. Clear guidelines like this make it easier to implement and enforce policies consistently across the organization.

Collaborating with Diverse Stakeholders

Ethical AI policies are strongest when they are informed by diverse perspectives. Engaging stakeholders from various backgrounds ensures your policies address potential blind spots and align with broader societal values.

For instance, involve representatives from your legal, technical, and marketing teams to ensure the policies cover compliance, implementation, and communication aspects. Additionally, consulting external experts, such as ethicists or industry advisors, can provide valuable insights and help refine your approach.

Employee Engagement and Feedback

Employees who interact with AI systems daily can offer practical insights that shape effective policies. Establish feedback loops that encourage employees to share their experiences, raise concerns, and suggest improvements.

For example, a retail company using AI for inventory management might solicit feedback from store managers who rely on the system. Their observations could reveal issues, like inaccuracies in demand predictions, that might not be apparent from a high-level perspective. By involving employees in the policy creation process, businesses foster a culture of collaboration and shared responsibility.

Rolling Out Policies and Ensuring Compliance

Once your ethical AI policies are defined, the next step is implementation. Start with comprehensive training programs that educate employees about the policies and their importance. Use real-world scenarios and interactive sessions to make the training engaging and relevant.

For instance, a training module for a small financial firm could include a case study on ensuring fairness in loan approvals, demonstrating how employees should handle sensitive customer data. Regular compliance checks, such as audits and performance reviews, ensure the policies remain effective and are consistently followed.

Adapting Policies Over Time

AI technologies and societal expectations evolve, and so should your policies. Establish a system for regularly reviewing and updating your ethical standards to keep pace with new developments.

For example, a business using AI for customer recommendations might revise its policies as new privacy regulations emerge, ensuring continued compliance. Regular updates demonstrate a commitment to ethical practices and help maintain trust with customers and stakeholders.

Inspiration from Industry Leaders

Look to industry leaders for examples of successful ethical AI policies. For instance, some tech companies have adopted transparency standards that clearly explain how their algorithms work, while financial firms have implemented strict data security protocols. These examples can inspire and guide your own efforts, helping you create policies that are both practical and aspirational.

By defining clear ethical standards, collaborating with stakeholders, and committing to continuous improvement, businesses can create a robust framework for ethical AI. In the next section, we'll dive deeper into data privacy and security, exploring how to protect sensitive information while maintaining customer trust.

Defining Your Ethical AI Principles

***Objective**: Identify and align your business's ethical priorities with actionable AI policies that support transparency, fairness, and accountability.*

1. ***List Your Ethical Priorities**: Write down three ethical principles that are most important to your business. These could include fairness, transparency, data privacy, inclusivity, or environmental sustainability.*
   ***Example**:*
   - *Fairness in hiring practices*
   - *Transparency in customer communications*
   - *Data privacy for all user interactions*

2. ***Align with Your Core Values**: For each priority, explain how it reflects your business's mission and values.*
   ***Example**: "Fairness in hiring aligns with our commitment to fostering diversity and equal opportunity in the workplace."*

3. ***Identify AI's Role in Supporting Each Priority**: Think about how AI tools can help uphold each ethical principle. Consider areas like bias detection, secure data handling, or increasing transparency.*
   ***Example**: "AI-powered tools like resume screening systems can help eliminate unconscious bias in hiring decisions."*

4. ***Draft a Policy Statement**: Write a one-sentence policy for each ethical priority, defining how your business will use AI responsibly to uphold these values.*
   ***Example**: "We will use AI-powered tools to ensure hiring processes are free from bias, fostering a diverse and inclusive workplace."*

5. ***Reflect and Share**: Share your draft policies with key stakeholders (e.g., your team or trusted advisors) for feedback and suggestions. This collaborative approach helps refine your policies and ensures they align with broader business goals.*

Outcome

By completing this exercise, you'll have a clear starting point for crafting ethical AI policies tailored to your business's needs. These policies will not only guide your AI implementation but also demonstrate your commitment to responsible innovation.

Implementing Ethical AI Practices

Objective: *Develop and enforce ethical AI policies that ensure transparency, fairness, accountability, and data privacy in your business operations.*

1. ***Define Your Ethical Priorities***: *Start by identifying the ethical values most important to your business. These should align with your core mission and societal expectations.*
   Example: *"Transparency, fairness, and data privacy are our top priorities for building trust with our customers."*
   Action Step: *Host a brainstorming session with key stakeholders to clarify your ethical goals.*

2. ***Conduct an Audit of Current AI Systems***: *Evaluate existing AI tools and processes to identify potential ethical concerns, such as biases, lack of transparency, or security vulnerabilities.*
   Example: *Review your AI-driven hiring tool to ensure it doesn't exhibit bias against certain demographic groups.*
   Action Step: *Use AI audit tools like Google's What-If Tool or IBM AI Fairness 360 to assess system behavior.*

3. ***Develop Clear Ethical AI Policies***: *Document your ethical principles and guidelines, ensuring they are actionable and aligned with industry standards.*
   Example: *Create a policy requiring transparency in customer-facing AI, such as disclosing when chatbots are used.*
   Action Step: *Write a code of ethics specific to AI usage and include it in employee handbooks.*

4. ***Implement Training and Awareness Programs***: *Educate your team on ethical AI practices and the importance of upholding these principles in daily operations.*
   Example: *Host workshops on recognizing and mitigating bias in data analysis.*
   Action Step: *Partner with organizations like AI Ethics Lab to design tailored training sessions.*

5. ***Establish Accountability Measures**: Assign roles and responsibilities for monitoring AI systems and enforcing ethical practices.*
   ***Example**: Appoint an AI Ethics Officer to oversee compliance and address concerns.*
   ***Action Step**: Set up a reporting system for employees or customers to flag ethical issues in AI use.*

6. ***Monitor, Review, and Adapt**: Continuously evaluate your AI policies and practices to ensure they remain relevant and effective as technology evolves.*
   ***Example**: Review your AI-driven marketing tools quarterly to ensure they comply with new data privacy laws.*
   ***Action Step**: Schedule regular ethics audits and update policies based on findings.*

As entrepreneurs integrate AI deeper into their operations, maintaining human oversight is only part of the equation. The next critical layer of trust comes from how responsibly data is collected, stored, and used.

12.4 Ensuring Data Privacy and Security

Ensuring Data Privacy and Security
AI systems rely on vast amounts of data, and trust depends on how that data is managed. Current standards such as **ISO 27001**, **SOC 2**, and **GDPR** set baselines for secure storage and processing. The **EU AI Act** extends these requirements by demanding clear documentation of datasets, model-training methods, and risk-mitigation steps.

Entrepreneurs should:

- Minimize data collection to what's truly necessary for the task.
- Use anonymization or pseudonymization to protect user identities.
- Disclose when customers are interacting with AI systems.
- Explore **privacy-preserving learning** (such as federated learning or differential privacy) when handling sensitive data.
- Schedule regular security audits to uncover vulnerabilities or bias.

Responsible data governance is no longer a box-checking exercise—it's a competitive advantage that demonstrates credibility to customers and investors alike.

Embracing Data Privacy Principles

Data privacy begins with understanding and applying foundational principles like data minimization and informed user consent.

- **Data Minimization:** Only collect the data you truly need for a specific purpose. For instance, a small online retailer should gather information relevant to order processing, such as name and shipping address, rather than unnecessary personal details.

- **User Consent:** Clearly communicate why you're collecting data and how it will be used, giving customers the ability to opt-in. For example, a fitness app might ask users if they're comfortable sharing their activity data for personalized coaching tips.

By adhering to these principles, businesses demonstrate respect for customer privacy and reduce the risks associated with excessive data collection.

Building a Digital Fortress: Data Security

Protecting the data you collect requires robust security measures that safeguard against breaches and unauthorized access.

- **Encryption:** Encrypt sensitive data to ensure it's unreadable without proper authorization. Think of it as converting your customer records into a secret code that only you can decipher.

- **Access Control:** Implement strict access policies to ensure only authorized personnel can view or handle sensitive data. For example, a small law firm might use role-based access controls to limit who can access client case files.

- **Regular Audits:** Conduct routine audits to identify vulnerabilities and ensure your systems remain secure. Treat these audits as health check-ups for your digital infrastructure, addressing potential risks before they become crises.

Learning from Real-World Data Breaches

Past data breaches serve as cautionary tales, highlighting the importance of proactive measures.

Case in Action

A well-known social media platform faced backlash after a data breach exposed millions of user profiles. The breach occurred because outdated software left vulnerabilities unpatched. As a result, the company revamped its security protocols and invested in advanced monitoring systems.

Lessons from such incidents emphasize the importance of keeping systems updated, employing advanced security tools, and maintaining a vigilant approach to data protection.

Industry-Specific Data Privacy Challenges

Different industries face unique challenges in protecting data:

- **Healthcare:** Patient records are highly sensitive and require compliance with regulations like HIPAA (Health Insurance Portability and Accountability Act) in the U.S. This means implementing end-to-end encryption, robust access controls, and thorough employee training.

- **Retail:** With the rise of e-commerce, protecting customer payment information is paramount. Retailers must secure checkout systems with advanced encryption and comply with standards like PCI DSS (Payment Card Industry Data Security Standard).

By understanding and addressing the specific challenges of your industry, you can create tailored solutions that safeguard customer data effectively.

Building Trust Through Privacy and Security

Strong data privacy and security practices are not just about compliance—they're about building trust with your customers.

When customers know their information is handled responsibly, they're more likely to engage with your business. For instance, a subscription box service that highlights its data protection measures on its website might attract privacy-conscious customers. Transparency about your security efforts builds confidence, turning data protection into a competitive advantage.

As we move forward, we'll explore the challenges of bias and fairness in AI, examining how businesses can address these critical issues to ensure equitable and inclusive outcomes for all.

Even the best-designed privacy measures can weaken over time as systems evolve. That's why continuous monitoring and regular auditing are essential to sustain long-term trust.

12.5 Tackling Bias and Ensuring Fairness in AI

Artificial Intelligence has the potential to revolutionize industries, but with this power comes the risk of perpetuating or amplifying biases embedded in the data used to train these systems. Tackling bias and ensuring fairness in AI are essential steps toward creating systems that benefit all users equitably and avoid unintended harm.

Understanding Bias in AI

Bias in AI arises when the data or algorithms reflect and perpetuate societal prejudices, leading to unfair outcomes. For instance, hiring algorithms have historically favored male candidates due to biased data, and facial recognition systems have shown higher error rates when identifying people of color. These biases undermine trust and fairness, turning innovative tools into sources of harm.

The Role of Fairness in AI

Fairness extends beyond mitigating bias; it ensures equitable outcomes for all users. An AI system can only be considered fair if it consistently delivers results that do not disproportionately disadvantage specific groups. For example, fairness in credit scoring algorithms ensures that decisions are based on financial behaviors rather than demographic characteristics.

Tackling Bias with Diverse Training Data

Imagine teaching a language model with only one regional dialect—it would struggle to understand other accents or vernaculars. Similarly, AI systems trained on narrow, unrepresentative datasets are more likely to produce biased outcomes. Ensuring diverse and inclusive training data is a cornerstone of mitigating bias and achieving fairness.

Practical Strategies for Reducing Bias

1. **Bias Audits**: Conduct regular audits to identify and address disparities in AI performance across demographic groups. This

proactive approach helps pinpoint areas where bias may creep in, enabling timely corrections.

2. **Algorithmic Transparency**: Build transparency into the AI pipeline by documenting how data is collected, processed, and used. Transparency promotes accountability and allows stakeholders to identify potential sources of bias.

3. **Blind Data Inputs**: Use anonymized or neutral data where possible to prevent algorithms from being influenced by sensitive attributes such as gender, race, or age. For instance, blind hiring systems remove personal identifiers from resumes, ensuring fairer evaluations.

4. **Fairness Metrics**: Adopt fairness metrics to evaluate AI outcomes. These metrics measure whether algorithms are providing equitable treatment and results across different groups.

Building Trust through Fairness

Promoting fairness in AI fosters trust with users and stakeholders. People are more likely to engage with systems they perceive as fair and inclusive. For example, financial institutions that prioritize fairness in credit assessments build stronger relationships with their customers, gaining loyalty and trust.

Real-World Examples of Addressing Bias and Ensuring Fairness

- **Hiring**: A major tech company identified biases in its recruitment AI, which favored male candidates due to imbalanced historical data. By overhauling the training process and introducing fairness metrics, the company achieved a more balanced hiring system.

- **Facial Recognition**: Developers of facial recognition technology improved accuracy across diverse demographics by expanding datasets to include a wider variety of skin tones and facial structures, addressing earlier criticisms of bias.

- **Healthcare**: Predictive healthcare algorithms have been redesigned to focus on equitable outcomes. By ensuring training data represents diverse populations, providers have improved diagnostic accuracy for underrepresented groups.

The Path Forward

Tackling bias and ensuring fairness are not one-time efforts but ongoing commitments. Businesses must continuously monitor and refine their AI systems, incorporating feedback from users and audits to stay aligned with fairness goals. By prioritizing fairness, AI can become a force for equity and inclusion, helping to bridge gaps rather than widen them.

12.6 Building Trust with Ethical AI

Trust is the cornerstone of every successful business relationship, and in the realm of AI, it emerges as the cumulative result of ethical practices. Transparency, fairness, and accountability, when applied cohesively, create a foundation for trust that resonates with users and stakeholders. Ethical AI practices aren't just theoretical ideals—they're the gateway to customer loyalty, market differentiation, and long-term success.

Trust as a Holistic Outcome

Trust in AI is not built overnight or through a single action. It stems from a systematic approach to ethical principles:

- **Transparency** fosters confidence by clarifying how decisions are made.
- **Fairness** ensures outcomes are inclusive and equitable for all.
- **Accountability** guarantees users have clear channels to resolve issues and understand who is responsible.

When these elements are combined, trust becomes the natural outcome of ethical AI systems. Businesses that prioritize these principles create deeper relationships with their customers, foster loyalty, and stand out as leaders in their industries.

Explainability: The Key to Trust

Explainability is essential for making AI accessible and understandable. Without it, AI can feel like a "black box," leaving users unsure of its decisions and hesitant to trust its outcomes. Businesses can demystify AI by adopting the following practices:

1. **Simplify Outputs**: Use user-friendly interfaces and plain language to make AI decisions digestible. For instance, a loan application system could provide a clear, actionable reason for

rejection, such as "insufficient credit history," instead of vague or technical explanations.

2. **Provide Context for Decisions**: Empower users with insights into why and how AI reached a conclusion. For example, an AI-powered hiring tool could offer a summary of skills or experiences that influenced its ranking of candidates.

These efforts reassure users that AI operates fairly and transparently, building trust through clarity.

Unified Trust-Building Framework

To systematically build trust, businesses can adopt a cohesive framework that integrates core ethical principles into every aspect of their AI systems. Here's a practical checklist for fostering trust:

- **Transparency**:
    - Share detailed but understandable explanations of how AI processes work.
    - Disclose data collection and usage policies clearly, empowering users to make informed decisions.
- **Fairness**:
    - Regularly audit AI algorithms to detect and address biases.
    - Use diverse datasets to ensure AI reflects the broad spectrum of user needs and experiences.
- **Accountability**:
    - Establish remedy mechanisms that allow users to report and resolve concerns.
    - Clearly communicate who is responsible for decisions and how users can escalate issues when necessary.

This framework helps businesses navigate the complexities of trust-building by addressing user expectations proactively.

Real-World Trust-Building Initiatives

Many industries are already showcasing how ethical AI fosters trust and innovation:

1. **Healthcare**: Hospitals leveraging AI diagnostic tools now provide detailed, patient-friendly reports explaining how results were derived. By combining transparency and explainability, these institutions enhance trust and improve patient engagement.

2. **Finance**: Banks are increasingly transparent about credit scoring criteria. By explaining the factors influencing loan approvals or rejections, they empower customers to take actionable steps to improve their financial standing.

3. **Retail**: E-commerce platforms use AI to personalize recommendations, but transparency in algorithmic processes reassures customers that their data is used ethically and securely.

Each example highlights how businesses can turn ethical principles into practical actions, creating trust and driving success.

The Business Advantage of Trust

Ethical AI is more than a moral obligation—it's a strategic asset. In an era where consumers value transparency and fairness, businesses that prioritize trust set themselves apart from competitors. Trust builds loyalty, attracts new customers, and safeguards against reputational risks. More importantly, it ensures that AI systems serve as a force for good, enhancing relationships rather than straining them.

As we move forward, keep in mind that trust is the linchpin of ethical AI. It's not a one-time achievement but an ongoing commitment to transparency, fairness, and accountability. By adopting these principles, businesses can navigate the complexities of AI responsibly, setting the stage for meaningful, long-term success.

AI Governance in Plain English

Regulations are evolving (e.g., the EU's AI Act) and most boil down to a few practical habits you can adopt now:

- ***Know your data.*** *Track sources and consent; prefer first-party data.*
- ***Label automated interactions.*** *Make it clear when customers are chatting with AI.*
- ***Keep a human in the*** *loop for important or sensitive decisions.*
- ***Document prompts & versions*** *for repeatability and audits.*

12.7 Summary

Ethical considerations are not just a responsibility but a strategic advantage in today's AI-driven world. This chapter explored the foundations of ethical AI practices, emphasizing the importance of transparency, accountability, and fairness. By tackling issues such as bias, data privacy, and trust-building, businesses can ensure their AI implementations are both effective and responsible.

We provided actionable steps for creating ethical AI policies, conducting audits, and fostering a culture of accountability. Through playbooks and exercises, you've learned how to identify your business's ethical priorities and align them with practical strategies. These tools empower you to implement AI solutions that reflect your values while meeting customer expectations.

Remember, ethics is not a one-time initiative—it's an ongoing commitment. As AI continues to evolve, so too must your approach to managing its impact. Trust isn't built overnight, but by prioritizing ethics at every stage of your AI journey, you're not just building a better business; you're shaping a better future.

In the next chapter, we'll delve into real-world case studies that illustrate how businesses across industries are implementing ethical and innovative AI solutions. These examples will inspire you to apply the principles learned here in your own unique way. Get ready to see ethics in action!

Chapter 13: Navigating Future AI Trends

Adapting Today for Tomorrow's Innovations

Artificial intelligence has moved beyond simple automation into a new era of **agentic AI** — systems that can plan, act, and learn toward goals with minimal human intervention. GPT-5 and its peers now support multimodal reasoning across text, images, audio, and even video, enabling businesses to build assistants that understand and operate in real-world contexts. The next wave of innovation isn't about replacing people, but augmenting them with autonomous collaborators that work alongside humans.

These advancements aren't just fancy ideas or distant possibilities—they're actively redefining industries, workforces, and everyday life. From quantum computing's unprecedented processing power to AI working alongside the Internet of Things (IoT) to create smarter environments, the future is unfolding at lightning speed.

This chapter takes you on a tour of emerging AI trends that are transforming our world. You'll explore technologies like edge computing, autonomous systems, and workforce shifts, with practical examples of how they're shaping industries. By understanding these trends, you can equip yourself and your business to adapt, innovate, and thrive.

The Only Constant is Change

AI is evolving faster than ever, and staying ahead isn't just about keeping up—it's about embracing change as an opportunity to innovate. Be the disruptor, not the disrupted!

13.1 Quantum Computing: Transforming AI

Quantum computing sounds like something straight out of science fiction, yet it's becoming an essential tool in advancing AI. Unlike traditional computers, which process information one step at a time, quantum computers harness the power of qubits—units that can exist in multiple states simultaneously. This enables them to tackle complex problems exponentially faster than classical systems.

Why Quantum Computing Matters for AI

AI thrives on computational power. Whether training machine learning models or analyzing massive datasets, speed and efficiency are critical. Quantum computing takes these capabilities to unprecedented heights.

- **Optimizing Logistics:** Imagine a delivery service trying to map the fastest routes for thousands of packages. Quantum computers can solve these complex routing problems in seconds, saving resources and boosting efficiency.

- **Accelerating AI Training:** Training AI models involves running countless simulations. Quantum computing shortens this time dramatically, allowing businesses to deploy smarter solutions faster.

- **Revolutionizing Research:** Fields like drug discovery and materials science benefit from quantum simulations, which can model molecular interactions with unparalleled precision.

Everyday Applications

Consider a global retailer optimizing its supply chain using quantum AI algorithms. By reducing transportation delays and fuel consumption, the company saves millions while minimizing environmental impact. Similarly, in healthcare, quantum-enhanced AI could speed up drug discovery, leading to faster treatment options for patients.

Challenges on the Horizon

Quantum computing is still an emerging field. Current systems are expensive, require controlled environments, and face limitations in scalability. However, partnerships between tech companies and research institutions are advancing the field, making it essential for businesses to stay informed and prepared for when quantum computing becomes more accessible.

13.2 AI-Driven Edge Computing: Intelligence at the Source

Picture a self-driving car that can process road conditions in real-time or a factory sensor that detects issues before they cause downtime. This is the power of edge computing, which brings AI's processing power closer to the source of data collection.

How Edge Computing Works

Traditional AI systems rely on the cloud, where data is sent for analysis before results are returned. Edge computing eliminates this lag by processing data locally on devices like cameras, sensors, or smartphones.

Advantages of Edge Computing

1. **Instant Responsiveness:** Edge computing's local processing means faster decision-making. For instance, a security camera that detects an intruder can alert authorities immediately without waiting for cloud-based analysis.

2. **Cost Efficiency:** By reducing the volume of data sent to the cloud, businesses lower bandwidth usage and operational costs.

3. **Privacy Protections:** Keeping data on-site reduces risks associated with transmitting sensitive information over networks.

Real-World Applications

- **Retail:** Smart shelves use edge computing to monitor inventory levels, automatically reordering stock before it runs out.

- **Healthcare:** AI-powered medical devices track patient vitals in real time, alerting doctors to abnormalities even in remote areas.

- **Manufacturing:** Sensors on production lines instantly adjust operations to improve efficiency and reduce waste.

13.3 Autonomous Systems: Redefining Industries

From self-driving cars to autonomous drones, the rise of autonomous systems is reshaping how we move, work, and live. These AI-powered machines perform tasks independently, using sensors and algorithms to navigate their environments.

Benefits of Autonomous Systems

- **Efficiency Gains:** Autonomous machines operate 24/7 without fatigue, increasing productivity while reducing costs.
- **Enhanced Safety:** Drones monitor construction sites, and robots inspect hazardous areas, reducing risks for human workers.
- **Scalability:** Companies can expand operations without significantly increasing overhead.

Examples in Action

- **Logistics:** Self-driving delivery vehicles reduce fuel costs and ensure on-time shipments.
- **Retail:** Automated checkout systems, like those in Amazon Go stores, allow customers to shop without waiting in lines.
- **Healthcare:** Surgical robots enhance precision, while autonomous hospital carts transport supplies efficiently.

13.4 AI and the IoT: Creating Connected Worlds

When AI joins forces with IoT, the result is smarter systems that anticipate needs, improve efficiency, and enhance user experiences. Imagine a thermostat adjusting itself to your preferences before you walk in the door or a factory where equipment schedules its maintenance.

Real-World Impacts

- **Smart Homes:** AI-powered IoT devices personalize lighting, temperature, and entertainment based on user behavior.
- **Industrial IoT (IIoT):** AI analyzes data from sensors on production lines, optimizing workflows and preventing equipment failures.
- **Healthcare:** Wearable devices track patient health, alerting doctors to changes before they become critical.

Challenges and Opportunities

While AI and IoT create exciting possibilities, businesses must address data security, compatibility issues, and scalability challenges to fully capitalize on their potential.

13.5 Shifting Workforce Dynamics

AI isn't replacing jobs—it's changing them. As automation takes over repetitive tasks, humans are freed to focus on creativity, problem-solving, and strategy.

New Opportunities

Emerging roles include AI Ethics Officers, tasked with ensuring fairness and accountability, and Human-AI Collaboration Designers, who create workflows that balance automation and human oversight.

Upskilling for Success

Businesses must invest in employee training, equipping teams with technical skills and fostering creativity and emotional intelligence. This ensures workers thrive alongside AI, not in competition with it.

Mapping Your AI Future

Objective: *Reflect on the emerging AI trends discussed in this chapter and identify actionable ways to integrate them into your business.*

1. ***Choose a Trend***: *Select one AI trend from this chapter that resonates with your business goals or industry needs.*
   Example: *A retail business might choose "Smart Shelves and IoT" to streamline inventory management.*

2. ***Envision Its Impact***: *Describe how this trend could transform your business operations, customer experience, or efficiency.*
   Example: *"Smart shelves could automate restocking, reduce errors, and improve customer satisfaction by ensuring products are always available."*

3. ***Assess Feasibility***: *Identify potential barriers to implementation, such as costs, technical expertise, or infrastructure requirements.*
   Example: *"We need to upgrade our Wi-Fi network to support IoT devices."*

4. ***Plan a Pilot Project:*** *Define a small-scale project to test the trend in your business. Outline the steps, resources, and metrics for success.*
   Example: *"Test smart shelf technology in one store, tracking inventory accuracy and customer feedback over three months."*

5. ***Set Goals and Metrics**: Determine what success looks like for your pilot project. Include both quantitative (e.g., cost savings, efficiency improvements) and qualitative (e.g., customer satisfaction) metrics.*
   ***Example**: "Achieve a 20% reduction in restocking errors and a 15% increase in inventory accuracy."*

***Outcome**: By completing this exercise, you'll have a clear vision for how emerging AI trends could impact your business and a roadmap for exploring their potential through actionable steps.*

Preparing for Future AI Trends

***Objective**: Equip your business to embrace and adapt to emerging AI technologies, ensuring you stay competitive in a rapidly evolving landscape.*

1. ***Identify Relevant AI Trends**: Research and select the AI trends most likely to impact your industry or business. Consider factors like market demands, customer needs, and industry shifts.*
   ***Example**: For a retail business, trends like smart shelves or AI-powered personalization might be critical.*
   ***Action Step**: Use tools like Google Trends or industry-specific reports to identify key innovations.*

2. ***Evaluate Your Current Readiness**: Assess your business operations, technology infrastructure, and workforce skills to determine your preparedness for adopting these trends.*
   ***Example**: Review whether your current technology stack can handle edge computing or IoT devices.*
   ***Action Step**: Conduct a SWOT analysis (Strengths, Weaknesses, Opportunities, Threats) focusing on AI readiness.*

3. ***Start Small with Pilot Projects**: Select one trend and implement a small-scale project to test its feasibility and impact.*
   ***Example**: Implement a chatbot for customer service to explore AI-driven engagement before scaling to more complex AI applications.*
   ***Action Step**: Set clear goals and KPIs (Key Performance Indicators) for the pilot project to measure success.*

4. ***Monitor Outcomes and Gather Feedback**: Analyze the results of your pilot project, focusing on its effectiveness, ROI, and potential scalability. Collect feedback from stakeholders, including employees and customers.*
   ***Example**: Track customer satisfaction scores and cost savings after introducing AI-powered chatbots.*
   ***Action Step**: Use tools like Google Analytics, HubSpot, or internal surveys to collect and interpret data.*

5. ***Scale and Innovate**: Expand successful projects across your business and explore other AI trends that align with your goals. Innovate continuously by staying updated on AI developments.*
   ***Example**: After a successful chatbot pilot, integrate AI into other areas, such as inventory management or personalized marketing.*
   ***Action Step**: Develop a roadmap for scaling AI implementations, prioritizing areas with the highest potential impact.*

Tips for Success

- **Stay Agile**: Be ready to adapt as AI technologies evolve. Flexibility is key to staying ahead.

- **Engage Your Team**: Involve employees in AI projects and provide training to ease the transition.

- **Collaborate with Experts**: Partner with AI specialists or consultants to bridge knowledge gaps and accelerate adoption.

13.6 The Rise of Agentic AI

Traditional AI tools respond to prompts. Agentic AI takes that a step further by executing multi-step goals on its own — researching information, sending emails, generating reports, or even launching marketing campaigns. These systems use feedback loops and internal reasoning to decide what to do next, allowing them to manage complex workflows with little supervision.

For entrepreneurs, this shift means learning how to **design goals and guardrails** instead of just crafting prompts. When an AI can take initiative, clarity and ethics matter more than ever. Defining what success looks like — and what actions are off-limits — becomes part of leadership.

13.7 Summary

In this chapter, we've explored AI's cutting-edge trends, from quantum computing to edge devices, autonomous systems, and IoT integration. These innovations are transforming industries and shaping how businesses operate.

By staying informed and embracing these technologies thoughtfully, you position yourself to thrive in the future. In the next chapter, we'll explore real-world case studies of businesses successfully navigating AI's challenges and opportunities, bringing these concepts to life.

Chapter 14: Comprehensive Playbooks

Transforming Ideas into Action with AI

AI tools are no longer simple assistants that generate text on command—they've evolved into collaborative systems that can reason, plan, and execute tasks. With modern versions of ChatGPT and similar models, entrepreneurs can build customized workflows, connect their AI to live data sources, and even delegate routine decisions to specialized GPT agents. These playbooks show how to translate those capabilities into practical business impact.

The Human-AI Partnership

Think of modern AI systems less like tools and more like team members. They can remember your goals, analyze new information, and act within defined boundaries—just like an intern who never sleeps. The key is to train them with clarity and keep them aligned with your standards.

In this chapter, you'll find a collection of playbooks that address critical business areas like understanding your audience, crafting impactful product launches, and streamlining workflows. Each playbook combines strategic insights with the power of AI tools like ChatGPT, Jasper AI, and Zapier, ensuring you have the guidance needed to implement AI solutions in a way that aligns with your business goals.

Custom GPTs & Team Workspaces

Many teams now deploy custom GPTs—chatbots tailored with your brand's voice, product facts, and approved workflows—and share them in a team workspace. The benefit: everyone prompts the same on-brand assistant, which improves consistency, cuts ramp-up time for new teammates, and reduces one-off mistakes. If your work involves repetitive tasks (such as support, QA checks, or campaign briefs), consider automating them with a reusable custom GPT.

These playbooks are more than templates—they're dynamic guides designed to evolve with your business. By following these step-by-step processes, you'll not only harness AI's potential but also gain the confidence to adapt and innovate as your needs grow.

So, let's get started. It's time to turn ideas into action and bring your business to the next level with AI-powered playbooks.

To illustrate AI in action, meet Bob, a small-town florist who thought "digitizing operations" meant turning flowers into pixels. Once he tried a few simple AI tools—automated replies for FAQs, inventory reminders, and a basic recommendation system—his shop ran more smoothly, and customers received faster, more personalized service. The lesson: you don't need a massive stack; a few targeted wins compound fast.

14.1 Customer Insights Report Playbook

This playbook guides you in creating a **Customer Insights Report** that evolves with your business. Designed as a "live" document, it captures essential insights about your customer's demographics, psychographics, motivations, and pain points. By keeping this report updated, you'll maintain a clear, accurate picture of your audience, helping you make informed decisions and drive sustained growth.

Step 1: Overview Prompt

To start the conversation, use this overview prompt to give ChatGPT context on your business or product before diving into each section.

I want to create a detailed Customer Research Report for my business. This report will include insights into my customers' demographics, psychographics, motivations, and pain points. Just say OK. We will hash out each of these insights in the following messages. To start, let me provide some context about my business or product: `[description]`.

Example Descriptions:

- **Personalized Pet Nutrition Service**: A subscription service that provides customized pet food based on individual pet needs.
- **Eco-Friendly Skincare Line**: A natural skincare brand that targets environmentally conscious consumers committed to zero-waste packaging and sustainable ingredients.
- **Freelance Design Platform**: An online platform that connects freelance designers with small businesses, offering design services on demand with a focus on affordability and quality.
- **Boutique Fitness Studio**: A high-end fitness studio that offers personalized training programs for busy professionals, focusing on holistic wellness and flexible scheduling.
- **Educational Subscription Box for Kids**: A monthly subscription service that delivers hands-on science and art projects for children, designed to spark creativity and learning through fun, educational activities.

Step 2: Exploring Each Section in Detail

In this step, you'll go through each customer insight area, using the main prompt to get broad insights and follow-ups to clarify or dig deeper if needed.

Section 1: Demographics

What are the typical demographics of my customers?

ChatGPT Response Example

For a personalized pet nutrition service, typical customer demographics might include age, income, education, location, household structure, and pet ownership characteristics.]

Follow-Up Prompts (if needed):

Can you expand on income levels and how they relate to purchasing habits?

Could you break down typical geographic preferences further, such as urban versus rural areas?

What trends might emerge based on household structure or pet ownership characteristics?

Note: ChatGPT often anticipates and answers follow-ups in its initial response. Use these follow-up prompts to explore details more deeply or address any aspects that weren't covered.

Section 2: Psychographics

Describe the psychographic profile of my typical customer, focusing on their values, lifestyle, and interests.

[For personalized pet nutrition, customers might value convenience and quality, lead busy lifestyles, and view their pets as family members. They often have interests in health, wellness, and ethical consumerism.]

Follow-Up Prompts (if needed):

What lifestyle traits might influence this audience's purchasing decisions?

What core values are most likely to resonate with this group?

What are some specific interests or hobbies that align with my product/service?

Section 3: Motivations

What motivates my customers to choose my product or service?

ChatGPT Response Example

Motivations might include a desire for high-quality, tailored pet food that addresses their pets' unique health needs, convenience, and alignment with their own values around pet care.]

Follow-Up Prompts (if needed):

"Could you explain the emotional or practical factors that might influence this decision?"

"What are some specific problems or needs my product/service addresses that could be motivating factors?"

"How might social or personal identity play into their motivations?"

Section 4: Pain Points

What common pain points do my customers experience that my product or service can help solve?

ChatGPT Response Example

[For personalized pet nutrition, pain points might include difficulty finding quality pet food, managing pets with special dietary needs, or skepticism around commercial pet food brands.]

Follow-Up Prompts (if needed):

Could you give examples of frustrations customers have when looking for [similar product/service]?
What are some common obstacles customers face in this market or industry?
How does my product/service alleviate these specific pain points?

Step 3: Compiling the Insights into a Final Report

Once each section is complete, ask ChatGPT to combine the refined insights into a single, cohesive Customer Research Report.

Using the insights we gathered on demographics, psychographics, motivations, and pain points, create a single Customer Research Report for my business. Please organize it into these four sections and summarize key points clearly.

This final report gives you a structured summary of your customer insights tailored to your business.

Step 4: Updating and Evolving the Report

As your business grows, revisit this report to keep it current and aligned with any shifts in your audience. Use prompts to explore new insights as needed.

Example Update Prompts:

Are there any recent trends or changes in demographics I should consider?
How might recent market developments affect my customers' motivations or pain points?
Have there been shifts in customer interests or values that would impact my psychographic profile?

Checklist for Creating and Evolving Your Customer Insights Report

1. **Start with the Overview Prompt**: Set the purpose and structure for the report with a clear initial prompt.
2. **Dive into Each Section**: Use targeted prompts for demographics, psychographics, motivations, and pain points.
3. **Use Follow-Up Prompts (as needed)**: Refine each section by asking detailed follow-up questions to gain deeper insights.

4. **Combine Insights**: Ask ChatGPT to create a unified Customer Research Report organized by section.

5. **Update Regularly**: Revise and update each section with fresh prompts as your business grows.

Once you've gathered insights, it's time to turn them into action with a strong launch plan.

14.2 Product Launch Strategy

Launching a new product can be daunting, especially when you want to ensure all aspects—from marketing to customer communication—are effectively covered. This Playbook will guide you through leveraging AI tools to brainstorm, refine, and execute a successful product launch. We'll explore how to use different AI tools like ChatGPT and Jasper AI to work together to bring your product launch to life.

AI Tools Involved:

- **ChatGPT**: Brainstorming and refining ideas for messaging and strategy.

- **ChatGPT, Leonardo.ai, or MidJourney for Image Generation**: Creating visuals to support the campaign. While ChatGPT offers integrated image generation, Leonardo.ai and MidJourney are excellent alternatives for unique artistic styles and high-quality visuals. Depending on your needs, you can choose the best fit for your campaign.

- **Jasper AI**: Polishing and creating effective marketing copy for different platforms. While ChatGPT can also generate marketing copy, Jasper AI offers additional, specialized features for more refined adjustments, such as specific tone settings, content length optimization, and targeted platform outputs, making it particularly useful for high-quality marketing campaigns.

- **Zapier**: Connecting everything to create automated workflows. ChatGPT can generate scripts or ideas for automation, but Zapier excels at executing and linking workflows across various platforms, ensuring that your product launch happens seamlessly without manual intervention.

Step-by-Step Guide

Step 1: Ideation Using ChatGPT

Start by brainstorming ideas for your product launch strategy. ChatGPT can help you explore various angles, from the target audience to the most compelling messaging points.

I'm launching a new line of eco-friendly handmade candles. Can you help me brainstorm ideas for a launch strategy?

ChatGPT provides several approaches, such as targeting environmentally-conscious customers through an online campaign focused on sustainability, creating partnerships with local businesses for in-person events, and offering early-bird discounts to email subscribers.

Follow-Up:

Can you break down how I could target eco-conscious customers on social media?

ChatGPT suggests creating educational content about sustainable living, incorporating influencer collaborations with eco-conscious personalities, and promoting user-generated content like photos of customers enjoying the candles in their homes.

Refinement Iteration: If an idea resonates, drill down further with ChatGPT.

What are some possible Instagram post ideas for the launch campaign focusing on sustainability?

ChatGPT Response Example:

Here is a series of ideas, including educational infographics about eco-friendly living, videos showing the handmade process, and posts about the sustainable materials used.....

Cross-Tool Synergy

Brainstorming with ChatGPT is like planting seeds, but don't stop there! By combining different AI tools, you'll watch those seeds grow into something beautiful. ChatGPT lays the foundation for creative thinking, and from there, you use specialized tools to bring those ideas to life. Think of ChatGPT as your idea machine and the other tools as the builders who make it happen.

Step 2: Creating Visuals with ChatGPT

Once you have a clear idea of the messaging, it's time to create visuals that reflect the brand's eco-friendly values. Here is a prompt for ChatGPT Image Generation:

Generate an image of a serene living room with handmade eco-friendly candles on a table featuring soft natural light.

ChatGPT Image Generation Example Output

Here is an image of a serene living room featuring handmade eco-friendly candles on a wooden coffee table, with soft natural light and a cozy, sustainable decor. Let me know if you need any adjustments!

Depending on your visual style needs, you can use the image generation feature in ChatGPT or explore other options like **Leonardo.ai** and **MidJourney**. Use the generated visuals across your launch materials—on social media, in blog posts, and in emails—to create a cohesive and visually appealing narrative around your product.

Step 3: Editing an Image with ChatGPT

Often, ChatGPT doesn't produce exactly what you want. In our case, we don't want a candle on the rug (fire hazard, of course!) To edit the image, just click on it, which will place you in edit mode.

Once in edit mode, press the Select button (which looks like this ), then select (or highlight) the part of the image you want to edit with the mouse.

Then enter a prompt like this:

Remove the candle that is on the rug.

ChatGPT Response Example

Here is the updated image where the candle on the rug has been removed, leaving only the candles on the table. Let me know if there's anything else you'd like to adjust!

Step 4: Polishing Content with Jasper AI

With the ideas from ChatGPT and the visuals from ChatGPT, it's time to craft polished marketing copy.

Copy Creation Prompt for Jasper AI

> *Write a compelling Instagram caption for an eco-friendly candle that emphasizes sustainability and a peaceful atmosphere. Include a call-to-action for visiting our online store.*

Jasper AI crafts a polished caption

> *Transform your space with the gentle glow of our eco-friendly handmade candles. Sustainably sourced, naturally beautiful. 🌿 Tap the link in our bio to learn more and light up your world in a sustainable way! #EcoLiving #HandmadeCandles #SustainableLifestyle*

Further Refinement

Use Jasper AI to adjust tone or style depending on the platform—e.g., making it more formal for LinkedIn or playful for TikTok.

Step 5: Automating the Launch with Zapier

Finally, integrate everything using automation to make the launch seamless.

Zapier Workflow: Set up a Zap to automate social media posts across platforms using the visuals from ChatGPT and copy from Jasper AI. Create another Zap to automatically send launch emails to your subscriber list as soon as the product goes live.

Bringing It All Together

Using AI isn't just about replacing human effort; it's about boosting creativity and execution speed. Imagine having a team of specialists at your fingertips—each one ready to step in and do their part to perfection. That's what combining tools like ChatGPT, and Jasper AI feels like. Together, they can take your product launch from idea to reality with fewer bottlenecks and more creativity.

Brainstorming Practice

Use ChatGPT to brainstorm a launch strategy for a different product, such as an eco-friendly pet accessory. What different approaches could you use to connect with pet owners?

Cross-Tool Experiment

Choose a product of your own, and follow the steps in this Playbook—use ChatGPT for ideation, generate visuals with ChatGPT Image Generation, refine content with Jasper AI, and automate with Zapier. Record how each tool contributes to the final outcome.

This Playbook showcases a holistic AI-powered product launch, using each tool to its fullest potential. It encourages readers to explore the benefits of combining AIs, illustrating how these tools complement one another to create a cohesive and well-rounded campaign.

Finally, these strategies only work when you deeply understand your customers — let's put it all together.

14.3 Understanding Your Customers

Scenario: Getting to Know Your Current or Potential Customers

Understanding who your customers are and what they need is critical to developing effective products, services, and marketing strategies. This Playbook will guide you through using AI tools to develop a deeper understanding of your customers, their preferences, their pain-points, and their motivations. You'll use ChatGPT for research and ideation, ChatGPT's image tools, and Zapier for integrating insights into actionable workflows.

AI Tools Involved:

- **ChatGPT**: Gathering initial ideas for defining customer personas and uncovering their needs.
- **ChatGPT, Leonardo.ai, or MidJourney**: Creating visual representations of your target customers or illustrating key personas for presentations.
- **Zapier**: Automating the process of integrating customer insights into CRM tools or marketing platforms for immediate use.

Step-by-Step Guide

Step 1: Brainstorm Customer Segments with ChatGPT

Start by brainstorming potential customer segments and personas. ChatGPT can help generate ideas for different customer types and their unique needs.

Prompt

> *Help me brainstorm different types of customers for my eco-friendly handmade candle business. What are their possible needs and interests?*

ChatGPT suggests several customer segments, such as eco-conscious millennials seeking sustainable décor, gift-givers looking for thoughtful, memorable presents, and wellness enthusiasts interested in aromatherapy and natural ingredients. Use ChatGPT for ideation, create visuals with ChatGPT's image tools, refine copy with Jasper AI, and automate tasks with Zapier.

Follow-Up Prompt

> *What are the motivations for each customer type?*

For eco-conscious millennials, motivations include environmental responsibility and supporting small businesses. For gift-givers, it's about memorable, meaningful items. Wellness enthusiasts are motivated by the calming benefits and natural ingredients.

Step 2: Create Visuals of Personas with ChatGPT (Image Generation, Leonardo.ai, or MidJourney)

Next, use image generation tools to create visual representations of your customer personas.

Prompt

> *Create an image representing an eco-conscious millennial who might buy eco-friendly candles. They are in a modern living space, showcasing sustainable decor.*

The AI generates visuals that capture the look and feel of this customer type, giving you a clearer idea of who you're trying to reach.

These visuals can be used in marketing presentations or shared with your team to ensure everyone understands the target audience.

Step 3: Develop Messaging for Each Customer Type with ChatGPT

Once you have identified and visualized your customer segments, use ChatGPT to develop targeted messaging that resonates with each type.

Prompt

> *Write a marketing message that would resonate with eco-conscious millennials buying our candles. Focus on sustainability and supporting small businesses.*

ChatGPT Response

> *Our handmade candles are crafted with sustainability in mind—using all-natural ingredients and eco-friendly packaging. By choosing Green Glow, you're not just getting a candle; you're supporting a movement towards a greener future.*

Refinement Prompt

> *Adapt the messaging for different platforms (e.g., more formal for email marketing, casual for Instagram posts).*

Step 4: Automate Customer Insights with Zapier

Use Zapier to integrate customer insights into your CRM or marketing platform to make it easier to take action on what you've learned.

Zapier Workflow: Set up a Zap to send information about customer segments and messaging directly to your marketing team or CRM tool, ensuring everyone is aligned.

Bringing It All Together

Using AI isn't about replacing human effort; it's about boosting creativity and execution speed. Imagine having a team of specialists at your fingertips—each one ready to step in and do their part to perfection. That's what combining tools like ChatGPT, and Jasper AI feels like. Together, they can take your product launch from idea to reality with fewer bottlenecks and more creativity.

Brainstorming Practice

Use ChatGPT to brainstorm a launch strategy for a different product, such as an eco-friendly pet accessory. What different approaches could you use to connect with pet owners?

Cross-Tool Experiment

Choose a product of your own, and follow the steps in this Playbook—use ChatGPT for ideation, generate visuals with ChatGPT Image Generation, refine content with Jasper AI, and automate with Zapier. Record how each tool contributes to the final outcome.

This Playbook showcases a holistic AI-powered product launch, using each tool to its fullest potential. It encourages readers to explore the benefits of combining AIs, illustrating how these tools complement one another to create a cohesive and well-rounded campaign.

Share Your Experience with AI!

Now that you've completed your journey into unlocking AI for entrepreneurial success, you're in the perfect position to inspire others. By leaving a short review, you can help more entrepreneurs discover how AI can transform their businesses and unlock endless possibilities.

Your honest feedback not only helps future readers embrace AI with confidence but also supports me in creating even more valuable guides to empower small businesses.

LEAVE A REVIEW!

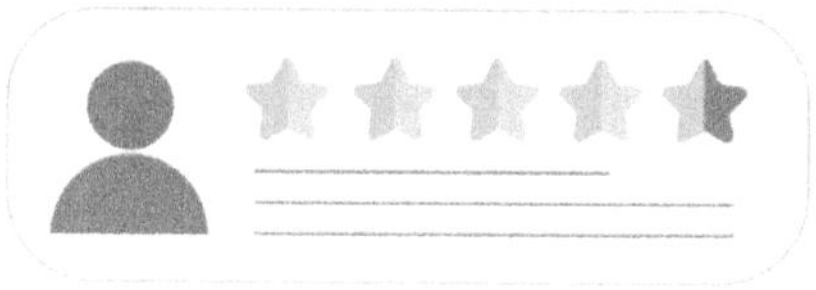

Thank you for taking the time to share your feedback—it means the world!

Scan this QR code…

Amazon Review
Unlocking Artificial Intelligence for Entrepreneur Success
https://www.amazon.com/review/create-review/?asin=1964520088

Conclusion

Unlocking AI's Potential for Your Business

Congratulations on completing your journey through **Unlocking Artificial Intelligence for Entrepreneur Success**! This book has been a roadmap to the world of AI, designed to empower you with practical tools, actionable strategies, and real-world insights tailored for small businesses and entrepreneurs.

Reflecting on the Journey

From demystifying AI's complexities to mastering conversational refinement with ChatGPT, we've explored how AI can transform the way you approach business challenges. We introduced tools to generate ideas, validate markets, optimize productivity, build sustainable practices, and enhance customer engagement. You've learned that AI isn't just for tech giants or coders—it's for anyone ready to experiment, innovate, and grow.

This book was designed as a practical guide, filled with exercises to build confidence, Nerd Nuggets to spark your curiosity, and playbooks embedded throughout the chapters to guide your strategic initiatives. Whether brainstorming a new product launch, automating customer service, or creating ethical AI policies, you now have a framework to adapt these lessons to your unique business needs.

Key Takeaways

1. **Start Small and Iterate**: As we discussed in the earlier chapters, small, focused steps lead to big outcomes. Whether crafting effective prompts or automating workflows, the key is to start, learn, and refine.

2. **Leverage AI as a Partner, Not Just a Tool**: AI isn't here to replace your creativity or hard work—it's a collaborative partner.

Let it amplify your strengths, tackle repetitive tasks, and uncover insights you might have missed.

3. **Embrace Change and Innovation**: The AI landscape is constantly evolving. As trends like quantum computing and autonomous systems become more accessible, staying informed and adaptable will position your business for long-term success.

4. **Focus on Ethics and Trust**: As powerful as AI is, its success relies on responsible use. By embracing transparency, fairness, and ethical practices, you can build trust with your customers and stakeholders.

Looking Ahead

The possibilities with AI are vast, but the real magic happens when you take action. This book has provided the tools and frameworks, but the next step is yours to take. Start with one idea, one tool, or one playbook, and watch how small changes ripple into transformative results.

As the world of AI continues to grow, so will the opportunities to innovate. Whether you're integrating AI into marketing, operations, or customer engagement, remember to remain curious, experiment boldly, and refine constantly. Success in the AI age isn't about perfection—it's about progression.

A Final Call to Action

Your journey doesn't end here. Use this book as a foundation to explore, experiment, and evolve your business strategies with AI. Share your successes, learn from setbacks, and keep pushing boundaries. Most importantly, stay committed to your vision and let AI be a partner in turning it into reality.

Your AI-powered future awaits. Let's unlock it together.

References

Services and Applications Mentioned in This Book

AI Ethics Lab - Ethical frameworks and tools for designing responsible AI policies and practices. https://aiethicslab.com

Asana - Task and project management platform with features like task assignments and project tracking. https://asana.com

Blue Prism - Robotic process automation tool for workflow automation and scalability. https://blueprism.com

Brandwatch - Social listening and analytics platform for monitoring trends and sentiment analysis. https://brandwatch.com

Browse AI - Web scraping and data extraction tool with automated data collection features. https://browse.ai

Buffer - Social media management platform for scheduling and analytics. https://buffer.com

Canva - Graphic design tool with templates and drag-and-drop features for creating professional visuals. https://canva.com

ChatGPT - Conversational AI platform for natural language generation and custom prompt crafting. https://openai.com/chatgpt

Clockwise - Time management and scheduling tool for optimizing calendars and meetings. https://getclockwise.com

Copy.ai - AI-powered content creation tool for copywriting and marketing materials. https://copy.ai

Customer.io - Marketing automation platform for customer segmentation and email workflows. https://customer.io

Excel - Data analysis tool with powerful spreadsheet, formula, and pivot table capabilities. https://microsoft.com/excel

Figma - Collaborative design tool for UI/UX design and prototyping. https://figma.com

Focus@Will - Productivity enhancement platform providing personalized focus music. https://focusatwill.com

Google Analytics - Web analytics tool for tracking traffic and user behavior. https://analytics.google.com

Google Looker Studio - Data visualization platform for creating reports and dashboards. https://lookerstudio.google.com

References

Google Sheets Forecasting Add-ons - Tools for advanced data forecasting in Google Sheets. https://workspace.google.com/marketplace

Google Trends - Search trend analysis tool providing real-time trend data. https://trends.google.com

Google Workspace - Collaboration suite with tools like Docs, Sheets, and Drive. https://workspace.google.com

HubSpot CRM - Customer relationship management platform with lead tracking and email marketing features. https://hubspot.com

IBM AI Fairness 360 - Open-source tool for detecting and mitigating bias in AI systems. https://aif360.mybluemix.net

Intercom - Customer communication platform with chatbots and live support. https://intercom.com

Jasper AI - AI content generation platform for blogs, social media, and marketing. https://jasper.ai

Leonardo.ai - Generative AI platform for creative design and art. https://leonardo.ai

MidJourney - AI-powered image generation tool for artistic and stylized designs. https://midjourney.com

Monday.com - Collaboration and project management platform with task tracking. https://monday.com

MonkeyLearn - Text analysis tool for sentiment analysis and topic classification. https://monkeylearn.com

Motion - Time and task management tool with automated scheduling features. https://usemotion.com

Notion - All-in-one workspace for notes, wikis, and project management. https://notion.so

Optimizely - A/B testing and website personalization platform. https://optimizely.com

Otter.ai - Transcription tool for automated meeting notes and recordings. https://otter.ai

Power BI (Microsoft) - Business intelligence platform for data visualization and analytics. https://powerbi.microsoft.com

Prisync - Price tracking and competitor analysis tool for pricing optimization. https://prisync.com

Qualtrics - Customer experience management platform with advanced surveys and analytics. https://qualtrics.com

Repustate - Sentiment analysis tool for text data with multilingual support. https://repustate.com

RescueTime - Productivity tracking tool for managing time effectively. https://rescuetime.com

Salesforce - CRM platform with automation and advanced analytics. https://salesforce.com

SEMrush - SEO and competitive analysis tool with keyword research capabilities. https://semrush.com

Shopify Reports - E-commerce analytics for sales and inventory tracking. https://shopify.com

Sprout Social - Social media management platform with scheduling and analytics tools. https://sproutsocial.com

SurveyMonkey - Survey creation and feedback collection platform. https://surveymonkey.com

Tableau - Data visualization tool for creating interactive dashboards and reports. https://tableau.com

Tidio - Customer support platform with chatbots and live chat features. https://tidio.com

Trello - Task and project management tool with boards and a drag-and-drop interface. https://trello.com

UiPath - Robotic process automation tool for automating workflows and integrations. https://uipath.com

Workable - Recruitment automation tool for hiring workflows and candidate tracking. https://workable.com

Zapier - Workflow automation platform for app integrations and task automation. https://zapier.com

Zoho CRM - CRM platform with sales automation and analytics. https://zoho.com/crm

Other Links of Interest

How Small Businesses Are Using AI—And How Yours Can ... https://www.forbes.com/sites/allbusiness/2023/11/17/how-small-businesses-are-using-ai-and-how-your-business-can-benefit-too/

How to Use ChatGPT for Business : Top 40 Applications https://research.aimultiple.com/chatgpt-for-business/

Top 10: No-Code AI Platforms https://aimagazine.com/ai-applications/top-10-no-code-ai-platforms

Success Stories: AI and Startups https://www.linkedin.com/pulse/success-stories-ai-startups-vishesh-saxena-2r2tc

References

Assessing AI Readiness: A Practical Guide for Companies https://www.fullstack.com/labs/resources/blog/ai-readiness-ai-development

Building an AI Literacy Program to Improve User Adoption https://clarkstonconsulting.com/insights/building-an-ai-literacy-program/

Top Generative AI Tools for Startups https://www.startupblink.com/blog/top-generative-ai-tools-for-startups/

5 Low-Cost AI Strategies for Your Small Business https://inclusioncloud.com/insights/blog/ai-on-a-budget-for-small-businesses/

9 Best AI Market Research Tools https://www.quantilope.com/resources/best-ai-market-research-tools

Best Predictive Analytics Software for Small Business in 2024 https://www.g2.com/categories/predictive-analytics/small-business

Top 15 Sentiment Analysis Tools to Consider in 2024 https://sproutsocial.com/insights/sentiment-analysis-tools/

AI-Driven Competitor Analysis: Redefining Market Strategy ... https://searchatlas.com/blog/ai-driven-competitor-analysis/

The 15 Best AI Tools for Small Businesses and How to Use ... https://blog.hubspot.com/sales/small-business-ai-tools

Scaling Customer Service with ChatGPT: The Success ... https://medium.com/@davidbrownie/scaling-customer-service-with-chatgpt-the-success-stories-of-industry-leaders-3b277f4583e8

AI Tools for Non-Technical Users https://redresscompliance.com/ai-tools-for-non-technical-users/

AI in Business: Enhancing Efficiency and Reducing Costs https://indatalabs.com/blog/ai-cost-reduction

AI Personalization Marketing: The Future of Customized ... https://www.eweek.com/artificial-intelligence/ai-personalization-marketing/

AI-Driven Customer Engagement: Strategies from Amazon, ... https://www.virtasant.com/ai-today/ai-driven-customer-engagement-strategies-from-amazon-nike-and-hilton

The Role of ChatGPT in Content Creation for Small ... https://medium.com/@rlyrlyrlyai/the-role-of-chatgpt-in-content-creation-for-small-businesses-d22d72af8d12

Top 10 AI Marketing Analytics Tools https://www.cmswire.com/digital-marketing/top-10-ai-marketing-analytics-tools/

A Business Guide to Responsible and Sustainable AI https://www.bsr.org/en/sustainability-insights/insights-plus/a-business-guide-to-responsible-and-sustainable-ai

10 Top Tools for Ethical AI Development 2024 https://dialzara.com/blog/10-top-tools-for-ethical-ai-development-2024/

How AI Will Accelerate the Circular Economy https://hbr.org/2023/06/how-ai-will-accelerate-the-circular-economy

Building a long-term AI strategy for your business https://www.ey.com/en_ie/ai/5-questions-to-help-you-build-a-long-term-ai-strategy

Five ways AI is helping small businesses succeed in 2023 ... https://ecapital.com/blog/five-ways-artificial-intelligence-is-helping-small-businesses-succeed-in-2023/

AI in Customer Service: Revolutionizing Digital Retail https://www.apu.apus.edu/area-of-study/business-and-management/resources/ai-in-customer-service/

How generative AI in agriculture could shape the industry https://www.mckinsey.com/industries/agriculture/our-insights/from-bytes-to-bushels-how-gen-ai-can-shape-the-future-of-agriculture

AI Adoption Challenges: Strategies for Successful Integration https://www.newhorizons.com/resources/blog/ai-adoption

AI Prompting Best Practices https://www.codecademy.com/article/ai-prompting-best-practices

ChatGPT for customer service: Use cases, prompts & limitations https://www.touchpoint.com/blog/chat-gpt-for-customer-service-prompts/

How to Automate Content Creation: A Step-by-Step Guide https://jetpack.com/blog/how-to-automate-content-creation/#:~:text=Automated%20content%20creation%20is%20the,templates%20or%20content%20management%20systems.

AI Process Optimization: What It is, Benefits & Examples https://www.pipefy.com/blog/ai-process-optimization/

AI Risk Management: Transparency & Accountability https://www.lumenova.ai/blog/ai-risk-management-importance-of-transparency-and-accountability/

Case Studies - Princeton Dialogues on AI and Ethics https://aiethics.princeton.edu/case-studies/

A Practical Guide to Building Ethical AI https://hbr.org/2020/10/a-practical-guide-to-building-ethical-ai

Addressing AI Bias: Real-World Challenges and How to ... https://www.digitalocean.com/resources/articles/ai-bias

References

Quantum Artificial Intelligence Is Closer Than You Think
https://www.forbes.com/sites/jonathanreichental/2023/11/20/quantum-artificial-intelligence-is-closer-than-you-think/

Generative AI and the future of work in America https://www.mckinsey.com/mgi/our-research/generative-ai-and-the-future-of-work-in-america

Navigating the nexus of AI and IoT: A comprehensive ...
https://www.sciencedirect.com/science/article/pii/S2542660524002592

The state of AI in 2023: Generative AI's breakout year
https://www.mckinsey.com/capabilities/quantumblack/our-insights/the-state-of-ai-in-2023-generative-ais-breakout-year

Made in the USA
Monee, IL
04 November 2026

67380797R00105